BACKWARD MASKING UNMASKED

Backward Satanic Messages of Rock and Roll Exposed

Jacob Aranza

HUNTINGTON HOUSE, INC.
1200 N. Market Street, Suite G
Shreveport, Louisiana 71107
(318) 222-1350

Third printing 1984
ISBN 0-910311-04-8
Library of Congress Catalog Card Number 83-080043

Printed in the United States of America

"Atmospheres are going to come through music because music is a spiritual thing of its own. You can hypnotize people with music, and when you get them at their weakest point you can preach into their subconscious whatever you want to say."
— Jimi Hendrix

"Rock and roll meant ——— (sexual intercourse) originally, which I don't think is a bad idea. Let's bring it back again." — Waylon Jennings

Dedication

This book is dedicated to Cleddie and Gayneil Keith who patiently loved me with the love of their Lord until He became my own.

Acknowledgment

Thanks to Theresa Lamson for typing the manuscript and to Rev. John Foster for taking pictures.

Letter from the Publishers

Dear Reader,

Welcome to *Backward Masking Unmasked,* by Jacob Aranza, a young evangelist from Lafayette, Louisiana.

Jacob — who is one of the finest young ministers in America — carries a heavy burden for the youth in this land. He is particularly concerned about the tragic influence rock and roll music has on young people.

Some of the material in this book will SHOCK you. You may find some of it objectionable and offensive.

We did.

But we agree with the author that the only way for America to wake up to the dangers of rock music is to tell it like it is.

The occult, witchcraft, Satan worship, homosexuality, perversion and drugs are all included in the lifestyles and the music of many of today's rock groups.

You could never really know the tragic truth about rock and roll music if we soft-pedaled the issue.

Nor would you ever know the truth about backward masking unless you receive a first-hand account.

Our prayer is that as you are enlightened on this subject you will fully understand the addictive nature rock music has on the youth of our land and the predictable consequences.

— The Publishers
Huntington House, Inc.

Introduction

The sinister nature of rock and roll music is one of the burning issues of our time.

Many of us remember the 1950's when this nerve-jangling sound swept across our country and around the world.

Today it has captured the attention and adulation of tens of millions of young people throughout the world.

Recent information concludes that rock stars are using a technique known as backward masking to implant their own religious and moral values into the minds of the youth of this and other lands.

"Backward what?" you may ask.

Backward masking.

Some reputable psychiatrists and psychologists are saying these satanic or drug-related messages can transcend the conscious and go directly to the subconscious part of a teenager.

What's so bad about that?

It depends on the message.

Jacob Aranza exposes what these messages in contemporary rock music include, messages such as the occult, Satan worship, drugs, sexual perversion and rebellion.

The backward masking messages closely parallel the life-styles of many of the rock musicians.

Jacob Aranza has done us all a great service by drawing this to our attention.

Why is it so important for us to know about rock music in general and backward masking in particular?

Because a recent national survey revealed that the average teenager in America listens to about six hours of music every day.

Thus, rock music certainly is one of the great vehicles for molding the morals of the youth of America.

Listen to what Jacob Aranza has to say. It will shock you, frighten you, enlighten you.

Hopefully all of us will be shocked, frightened and enlightened enough to make us want to do something about it.

— Bill Keith, Senator
The State of Louisiana

Contents

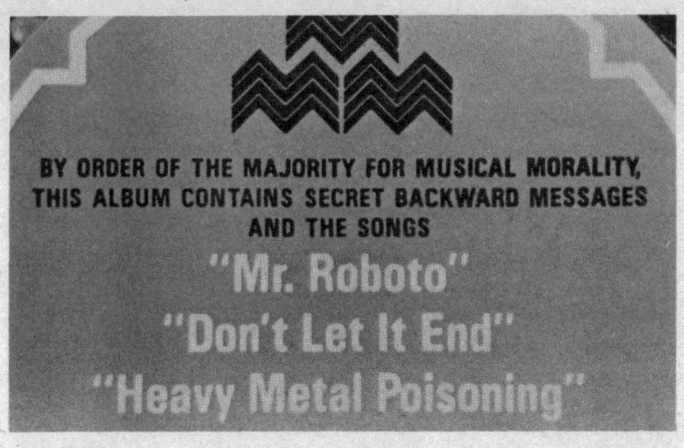

This is the front of the latest *Styx* release, an open admission to the use of backward masking.

Chapter 1

Backward Masking

What's wrong with Rock and Roll? Plenty! It affects tens of millions of young people and adults in America and around the world. Rock music is laced with lyrics exalting drugs, immorality, homosexuality, violence and rebellion. As if this wouldn't be enough, there is now a more sinister danger. It's called *backward masking.* Backward masking is a phrase created to describe a technique that rock groups are using to convey satanic and drug related messages to the subconscious. This technique is used by someone saying something forward which intentionally means something else played backward. Another way this can be used is by taking one of the many tracks that are used in recording an album and placing one secret message mixed into the album at a very low level, yet still backwards.

Now that you know what backward masking is you might wonder, "What does that have to do with me? I don't listen to my records backward."

Recent studies have been done by experts in the field of

the Subliminal and Subconscious Suggestion. One man who has been in the forefront of these studies is William H. Yarroll II, President of Applied Potentials Institute. His studies concluded that "at the base of the brain there is a 'check valve,' the Reticular Activating System. Based on prior programmed values, emotional responses, and our conditioning, a message will be accepted or rejected. If the sound presented is unfamiliar, it passes on for further examination and consideration. Part of the screening process involves comparison with known, or familiar, linguistic messages. If this interpretive process fails to match the message in the logical, conscious brain hemisphere, it is passed on into the next hemisphere (or part of the brain), for further evaluation. If the left conscious brain can find no known matching information, the creative right brain takes over the decoding process. As the right hemisphere mirrors the strange message, if it discovers the same phrase, the message is acknowledged and stored. Note that if a previous message (contrary to this one) has already been stored hundreds of times, it is doubtful that the formation of one new 'thought unit' would compel you to think this way. However, if you were to listen and decode the new message frequently enough, the new memory storage would eventually increase in size and concentration and become translated into 'reality.' The mind's check valve, the Reticular Activating System, screens or blocks out much unnecessary or 'invalid' information. An example of unnecessary information is the contents of the conversation going on around you in a busy restaurant, except when your name happens to be mentioned! The mind literally 'selects' what it chooses to consciously hear and focus on." *Rock Music and the Brain,* William Yarroll.

What Mr. Yarroll is actually saying is that if someone said to you, "Satan is God," you would immediately reject it or your "check valve," the Reticular Activating System would reject it. But if you heard, "dog si natas" a number of times, which is "Satan is God" backwards, it would be "decoded" by the right part (or creative part) of the brain and stored as fact!

Another man who has researched subliminal messages and their effect upon the emotions is Dr. Lloyd H. Silverman, adjunct professor at New York University. In the May, 1983 issue of *Psychology Today,* the renouned magazine highlighted Dr. Silverman's studies. "To date, he calculates, some 50 studies have demonstrated that the subliminal presentation of emotional charged messages can trigger unconscious thoughts and feelings, and thus alter behavior." The article goes on to say in 1956, a man by the name of James Vicary, a market researcher, claimed that science had proven the power of subliminal advertising to influence people's buying and selling habits. "Vicary announced that after he had repeatedly flashed the words POPCORN and DRINK COCA COLA on the screen in a movie theater, sales of the products went up 59 percent and 18 percent respectively."

According to the magazine, Dr. Silverman says that "subliminal perception" — the perception of stimuli too weak to be consciously recognized — is a real phenomenon that "has been demonstrated beyond any reasonable doubt."

Dr. Lew Ryder, a well-known psychiatrist, has studied the subject of the Power of Suggestion for many years. He says there have been many psychiatric tests made concerning the relation of suggestion and the subconscious. According to Dr. Ryder, this is how it works. "Tests have been made to determine audience response. During a (TV) program, a certain number would appear only briefly on the screen. It would not even be visible to the naked eye. Yet under hypnosis, the person who saw the film could recall the number. The conscious did not know about it, but the subconscious did!" "The real danger is the subliminal suggestion that violence and sexual freedom are normal," Dr. Ryder said. Yet another doctor, asked about the subliminal effects of backward masking, said, "Can the mind understand a subliminal message and then be affected by it? It's entirely within the realm of the neurophysiologically possible; at least a short message." He is Dr. Hal Becker, President of Behavioral Engineering in Metairie, Louisiana. For anyone who has had any experience with the occult, this is not shocking information about the backward satanic messages. Is it any wonder that in a recent TV interview that Jim Steinman, or as he is commonly called, "Meat Loaf," admitted that groups used backward masking, but only for fun? David Bowie even admitted in a recent *Time* magazine interview that one of his songs on his album "Lodger," was another song, just played backwards. The group "Styx," on their latest release have a label on the album stating, "This album contains backward masking" (see page 1). Of course, backward masking is nothing new to either of these groups.

While speaking recently with Jeff Pollard, former lead singer of the nationally known rock group "Louisiana LaRue," also the one who lead Kerry Livgreen of the rock group "Kansas" to Christ; he stated a view of backward masking that I very much agree with. Some groups that have backward masking on their albums or songs don't realize that though they have not intentionally placed backward satanic messages in their music, they are simply "pawns" in the hands of Satan. Serving Satan, we must remember, is not falling on our knees and worshipping him only. It can be simply serving ourselves.

When we really begin to think of the effect music has created in different eras of history and the fads and styles it has produced, then we will begin to consider more carefully what we listen to; because it will eventually determine our thinking and our perspective of principles and values.

If you don't think this music is affecting the values of young people then listen to a few letters that were written in response to the subject of backward masking being used satanically by rock groups. These letters were taken out of *Hit Parader* magazine. *Hit Parader* is a very popular rock magazine read by young people between the ages of 8 to 18:

"In a recent *Hit Parader,* a couple of your readers wrote about rock bands and satanism. Big fricken deal! They listened to Stairway to Heaven backwards. I've heard it too, but I still listen faithfully to Led Zeppelin."

— Gary Walker
Port Angeles, Washington

"All these Satan/Rock comparisons are driving me up a wall. I'm a good Catholic, but I also love rock."

— Stan Lapinski
Naples, Florida

"We are writing about a letter in a recent *Hit Parader.* These girls wrote in about how you could hear praise for Satan if you played records like Kiss, AC/DC, and Led Zeppelin backwards. We are pretty sick of hearing this. We have never heard this ourselves but even so, let them think what they want — rock is the best!"

— Lisa R. & Jill L.
Cape May, New Jersey

"The people who say that rock and roll music and the various groups are devil worshippers are ignorant, and don't know what rock music is all about. It's just music! It relieves people from all the everyday problems. If anything, it helps people."

— Steve Crocker
Orange Park, Florida

You can plainly see that backward masking and the forward messages of rock have taken tremendous toll already by the responses of these young people. The statement they are making is clear, "Don't confuse me with the facts."

The following chapters will begin to expose those that are using backward masking, how it began, its tie-in with the occult, and other groups' satanic life-style.

So hold on to your earphones, here we go!

CHAPTER 2

In the Beginning

The *Beatles* started using backward masking on their *White Album* with the song "Revolution Number Nine." The song repeatedly says "Number nine, number nine, number nine. . . ."

Played backwards it becomes "Turn me on, dead man; turn me on, dead man. . . ." Why? At this time the *Beatles* were trying to make the public believe that Paul McCartney was dead, merely as a publicity stunt. To reinforce this idea they placed a car on the front cover of the *Abbey Road* album. It was in the background with a license plate that read "28 if." This was to imply that Paul would be 28 years old if he were alive.

On the front of the album the *Beatles* appear to be dressed for and going to a funeral, except for Paul. He's the only one without shoes on.

Another segment on the same album sounds like a crowd making noise and someone screaming out "rape!" Played backwards it becomes "Let me out, let me out, let me out . . ." indicating that Paul was crying out from the grave. Then, between the songs "I'm So Tired" and "Blackbird," there's a gibberish kind of sound. Played backwards this says, "Paul is a dead man. Miss him, miss him, miss him."

Others who began to use the backward masking technique, whether knowingly or unknowingly, had other purposes in mind. Many anti-Christ statements can be found backmasked into songs, effectually attacking the faith of masses of young people.

Black Oak Arkansas on their album *Live Raunch and Roll* have a song entitled "When Electricity Came to Arkansas." On this particular song, the lead singer makes the sounds like a lot of people are screaming and growling. Played backwards it becomes "Satan, Satan, Satan. He is God, he is God, he is God."

Another group, the *Electric Light Orchestra,* had an album called *Face the Music.* At the very beginning of the song "Fire on High" there are weird sounding noises which make no sense played forward. Played backwards they become "The music is reversible but time is not. Turn back, turn back, turn back." They are informing the listener that their music is reversible and can be played backwards. They also backward masked anti-Christ statements on their *Eldorado* album.

Queen, a group who's name is often used in slang to mean homosexual, had a hit song entitled "Another One Bites the Dust." The segment in which they sing that chorus, when played backwards, says "Decide to smoke marijuana, marijuana, marijuana."

The group called *Styx* derived their name from the legendary river that flows through hell. A song of theirs entitled "Snowblind," when played in reverse, says "Satan, move in our voices."

Bob Garcia, of A&M Records in Los Angeles, said, "It must be the devil putting messages on the records because no one here knows how to do it."

Whether Bob Garcia knows how to do it or not doesn't discount what the messages are clearly saying. The *Beatles* knew how to do it. The *Electric Light Orchestra* knew how to do it as well as *Led Zeppelin!* It's hard to believe that none of these groups are aware of these messages, especially with their connections with the occult and the supernatural.

After I finished doing a radio program on backward masking one evening, a man called me and was very angry. He had heard what I said about backward masking and was insulted by what I'd said about his favorite group. And even though he heard these backward messages he still didn't believe it.

That's exactly what Satan wants us to believe. Because as long as we'll ignore him and the tools that he is using, he can continue to proclaim his message. The scriptures say, "My people are destroyed for lack of knowledge."

It is time we realize what we've been ignoring in the subtle messages of rock and roll from the time of Gene Vincent and Elvis Presley to the present day. There really is more to music than meets the ear!

Top: **The *Beatles* employed the technique of backward masking in their *Abbey Road* album. A picture on the album showed Paul McCartney (back) without shoes. *Bottom:* The *Queen's* top song "We Are the Champions" is the unofficial national anthem for gays (homosexuals) in America.**

Top: Aleister Crowley's book *Magick* teaches backward masking as a practice of the occult. *Bottom:* On the back cover of the *Beatles'* album *Sergeant Pepper's Lonely Hearts Club Band* is a picture of Crowley (second from left at top).

Chapter 3

The Missing Link

Edward Alexander Crowley (Aleister Crowley), 1875-1947, was the son of wealthy Plymouth Brethren parents. He was educated at Malvern, Tonbridge, Trinity and Cambridge colleges. He traveled widely through Europe and Asia and was very involved in Black Magic and the occult in the late 1800's. He was called the Beast, 666, and many called him the meanest man who ever lived. Crowley held sacrificial ceremonies at his mansion which allegedly included human bodies.

The importance of this information is in his link to backward masking and the occult. In our chapter entitled "In the Beginning" we said the *Beatles* were the first known users of backward masking. On the cover of their *Sergeant Pepper's Lonely Hearts Club Band* album, we find a sea of many faces. In the midst of them can be found the face of Aleister Crowley.

"We just thought we would like to put together a lot of people we like and admire," recalls Ringo Starr.[1]

Led Zeppelin's Jimmy Page is a devout follower of the teachings of Aleister Crowley and presently lives in the former occultist's mansion known as the Boleskine House.[2]

Page has turned the mansion into a shrine to Crowley and the occult. He has even commissioned avowed satanist Charles Pace to decorate his home in a motif depicting various forms of ritualistic magic. This mansion features an underground passageway where Crowley held his sacrificial ceremonies. This same passageway now leads to his grave. It is said that Crowley's ghost haunts the mansion and Page frequently tries to contact him through seances and spiritual readings.

Herein lies the connection: In Aleister Crowley's book *Magick,* one of his occultic teachings is that you should learn to talk backwards, write backwards, and play phonograph records backwards. This inspired and encouraged the use of backward masking in the record industry and directly tied it to the occult. This was to become a channel for satanically infiltrating the minds of unsuspecting people!

Popular rock star David Bowie is known to have said he purchased a record player to play records backwards because he believes songs from his *Young Americans* album resemble Tibetan spiritualistic chants.[3]

In a 1976 interview, he said, "Rock and roll has always been the devil's music. It can well bring out a very evil feeling in the west."[4]

Former rock star Little Richard, who has since become a preacher of the gospel, relates, "Some rock and roll groups stand around in a circle and drink cups of blood. Some get on their knees and pray to the devil. Rock and roll hypnotizes us and controls our senses."[5]

Jimi Hendrix spoke openly about the spiritual aspect of music when he said, "Atmospheres are going to come through music because music is a spiritual thing of its own. You can hypnotize people with music, and when you get

Ozzy Osbourne paid tribute to Crowley in his best-selling album *Blizzard of Ozz*.

Osbourne's *Diary of a Madman* shows the upside down cross, a symbol of the occult. Osbourne also performs other occultic, ritualistic acts during his performances.

them at their weakest point you can preach into their subconscious whatever you want to say."[6]

Aleister Crowley may have died in 1947, but the evil he began continues with us to this day. The same spirit that many years ago inspired him is still alive in those who pursue his ideology and life-style.

The *Beatles* and *Led Zeppelin* are not the only rock groups that have dared to identify with Crowley. Daryl Hall also claims to be a follower of his teachings[7] and openly admits he's "into witchcraft."[8] Ozzy Osbourne, formerly of the group *Black Sabbath* whose music is called by many "Satan Rock" wrote a song on his album *Blizzard of Ozz* titled "Mr. Crowley," in dedication to him. Osbourne claims he was compelled to see the movie *Exorcist* 26 times.[9] He also said, "I don't know if I'm a medium for some outside source. Whatever it is, frankly I hope it's not what I think it is, 'SATAN!' "

Osbourne recently received precautionary treatment for rabies after biting the head off of a bat at a concert![10]

Ritchie Blackmore, formerly of *Deep Purple* and now with his own group named *Rainbow,* admits he has "regular seances to get closer to his god." While he performs he astro-projects out of his body and floats around the concert hall.[11] He supposedly records in a 17th-century castle haunted by a demon who is a servant of the 4,000-year-old Babylon god called Baal. He has songs like "A Black Magician," "Stargaze" and "Tarot Woman" which are written about the predictions of the tarot cards.

Mick Jagger of the *Rolling Stones* said, "There are Black Magicians who think we are acting as unknown agents of Lucifer." He also said that Anton LaVey (founder of the first satanic church and author of the Satanic Bible) has helped to inspire their music as he did with the song "Satanic Majesties Request," the unofficial anthem for all satanic churches.[12]

Newsweek Magazine calls Mick Jagger "The Lucifer of Rock, the Unholy Roller," and said that his demonic power affects people.[13]

Keith Richards of the *Stones* said, "The *Stones'* songs come spontaneously like an inspiration at a seance." He goes on to say, "The tunes arrive 'en masse' as if the *Stones* as songwriters were only a willing and open medium."[14] With songs like "Dancin' with Mr. D" not much is left to the imagination. You don't have to look and listen long to see the open satanic emphasis of this group.

What the devil's wrong with rock and roll? The devil is what's wrong with rock and roll and there's no secret about it! There's a revival going on in Satan's kingdom and music is his tool.

[1]*Hit Parade,* October 1976, p. 14

[2]*Hit Parade,* July 1982, p. 7

[3]*Hit Parade,* July 1975, p. 16

[4]*Rolling Stone,* February 12, 1976, p. 83

[5]*Harrisburg Patriot News,* Summer 1980

[6]*Life Magazine,* October 3, 1969, p. 74

[7]*Circus,* October 13, 1977, p. 28

[8]*Sixteen,* May 1981, p. 26

[9]*Circus,* February 1976

[10]*Waco Tribune-Herald,* January 28, 1982

[11]*Circus,* August 16, 1976, p. 30

[12]*Rolling Stone,* August 19, 1971

[13]*Newsweek,* January 4, 1971, p. 44

[14]*Rolling Stone,* May 5, 1977, p. 55

Anton LaVey, the author of the *Satanic Bible,* is well-known among rock and roll stars. These pictures appeared on the back of the *Satanic Bible.*

Chapter 4

Witch Way Are the Eagles Flying?

With songs like "Witchy Woman" and "One of These Nights" which says, "You've got your demons; you got your desires; I've got some of my own. I've been searching for the daughter of the devil himself," one hardly needs to look to see the occultic lyrics they write.

The *Eagles* have enjoyed much success in recent years. One of their latest hits was "Hotel California" which stayed on the charts for several months. Part of the song says, "There she stood in the doorway; I heard the mission bell and I was thinking to myself this could be heaven or this could be hell. Then she lit up a candle and showed me the way. There were voices down the corridor. I thought I heard them say, 'Welcome to Hotel California, such a lovely place (such a lovely face).' "

The only phrase in parenthesis in the whole song is the one you see above. If you were to open the album and look on the inside cover (see page 20), you would see three windows on the far left hand side. In the middle window, if you look very closely, there is a man's face who resembles Anton S. Zandor LeVay. He is the founder of the church of Satan and is called the Black Pope by many of his followers. He is also the author of the first Satanic Bible.

Is this just an accident? Hardly!

While on a recent speaking tour we went to San Francisco looking for the satanic church and found the street where they used to meet. It's California Street! The fifth stanza of the song says, "So I called up the Captain, please bring me my wine. He said, 'We haven't had that spirit here since 1969. . . .' "

May I remind you that wine is symbolic of the Holy Spirit in Christianity and he said they hadn't had that spirit there since 1969! In 1969 the Satanic Bible was copyrighted and released. The last stanza says, "Last thing I remember I was headed for the door. I had to find the passage back to the place I was before. . . .'Relax,' said the night man, 'we are programmed to receive. You can check out anytime you like but you can never leave.' "

Still think this is all coincidence? One segment of the song played backwards says, "Yes, Satan organized his own religion."

Eagles' manager, Larry Salter, has admitted that members of the group had dealings with members of the satanic church.[1]

According to a Dallas evangelist who said he talked with Salter about the group:

"The *Eagles* got their name from the Major of the Indian Cosmos and many of their songs are nurtured by the drug peyote as well as being based on the teachings of Carlos Castenada, under whose occultic writing the band was formed."[2]

The songs that the *Eagles* are singing and the direction in which they are flying may surprise you, but those who have listened to these lyrics should not be caught by surprise. I believe the philosophy of the group can best be summed up in their own words from their *On the Border* album. These are a few words from the song "Good Day in Hell!" "In that good book of names I wanna go down in flames, seeing how I'm going down. Oh well, it's been a good day in hell, tommorrow I'll be glory bound."

Whether the *Eagles* will ever be glory bound is certainly questionable, but one thing is sure, "Hotel California" is not a place where you and I should spend any day or night! This Southern California group's country-rock blend may at first sound harmless. But continued listening could become harmful. Don't forget, BIRDS OF A FEATHER FLOCK TOGETHER!

[1]*Waco Tribune-Herald,* February 28, 1982

[2]*Time,* August 15, 1975, p. 4

Chapter 5

Rock History

If I were to come into your home and tell you to worship Satan, I wonder what your response would be. I presented this question to a crowd of young people I was to speak to about rock and roll. Their response was one of complete shock. It sounded as removed from rock and roll as the subject of sex might seem. Yet sex is just as related as Satan is to rock and roll.

In 1954 a Cleveland disc jockey by the name of Alan Freed was searching for a name to best describe a new music fad pioneered by such men as Gene Vincent, Chuck Berry and Elvis Presley. Freed finally found a name he borrowed from the ghetto term describing premarital sex. The name was rock and roll. Many have since forgotten Alan Freed, but rock and roll has lived on.

While speaking in public schools in the Midwest recently, I began to take a poll of how much time students spend listening to radio. The average was three to five hours a day. I asked them, "If I were to train you to think like me for one hour a day, after a year would you think somewhat like me?" All agreed they probably would.

If this is true, the greatest influence on the teenage minds in America today is not school, parents or books, but music. How many times have you driven down the street and begun to sing one of the top ten songs, not even realizing you knew the song? And 75 percent of the rock and roll you would be singing today deals with sex, evil, drugs and the occult.

Just like others today who once loved rock and roll but are now exposing the real message in rock, I was also naive and ignorant. If that's where you are today, but are searching, don't be turned off by opinions you may have heard in the past.

I, too, have been stopped by the well-meaning adult who looked at me with all the spirituality possible and said, "Young man, that rock music is from the devil! Those loud guitars and that jungle beat are from the pit of hell! You stay away from that stuff!"

At a high school crusade in California where I spoke I was encouraged to hear of a 17-year-old student who told his teacher afterwards, "Many people have come and given us their opinion on rock, but finally we have heard the facts!"

Just take a look at the changes of rock since its birth in the 50's. People, who were at one time appalled by the shocking hips of Elvis, would soon be shocked out of their wits in the early 60's by the *Beatles* who were to declare that they were more popular than Jesus Christ!

Just when we were all getting used to the *Beatles,* we were shocked again by the likes of Jimi Hendrix and Janis Joplin.

Janis summed up her ambitions in statements like, "I want to smoke pot, take dope, lick dope. Anything I can get my hands on I want to do. All my life I just wanted to be a beatnik, meeting all the heavies, get stoned, (——————) and have a good time."[1]

Amazingly enough the worst was yet to come with people like Alice Cooper, a Mormon preacher's son who claims to be a reincarnated witch from the seventeenth century. He gave his audiences exhibitions of transvestism.

Alice was quoted as saying, "Rebellion is the basis for our group. Some of the kids who listen to us are really deranged, but they look up to us as heroes because their parents hate us so much."

But Alice was just scratching the surface compared to *KISS* (Kids In Satan's Service) which was to become a household word. Rock and roll magazines call them the "Fire breathing demons from rock and roll hell."[2]

Former member Peter Criss declares, "I find myself evil. I believe in the devil as much as God. You can use either one of them to get things done."[3]

Gene Simmons of the group says, "I've always been interested in what human flesh tasted like, and I have always wanted to be a cannibal." He adds, "If God is such hot stuff then why is he so scared to have other gods before him? I've always wanted to be God."[4]

Marvel Comics produced a special edition dedicated to *KISS*. Blood samples were taken from the group and smeared on the plates so they could say, literally, that the comic was printed in the blood of the band. *Marvel* editor Steve Gerber aimed the magazine directly at eight- to nine-year olds.

Still the road to rock would be paved with many other groups to come. Everyone waited. What next?

I was in Europe in 1978 and saw the new beginning.

I was speaking in an open market place in England when, in the middle of my message, a teenager came and stood across from me. I tried not to stare, but it was difficult. His hair appeared like a long crew-cut. It stuck straight up in the air, uneven and jagged in many places. I had never seen anyone with safety pins stuck in their face before, or leopard-skin pants on. Maybe it was the pink, red, orange, blue and blond hair that caught my attention the most.

After I finished speaking he walked over to me and said, "Hey, what's wrong with you man?"

I couldn't believe it! Here he was with his hair dyed six different colors, safety pins in his face, leopard-skin pants on, his hair jagged and nappy looking and he was asking what was wrong with me!

This was my first encounter with what was to come. Namely, Punk Rock. When I found out what he represented I laughed to myself and said, "The kids in America will never go for this!" But they did!

So here we are, after 25 years of rock and roll. Who knows what's next? I certainly don't! But this I do know: if it follows the trail of its predecessors it will be louder, ruder and lewder.

[1]*Time,* August 9, 1969, p. 76

[2]*American Photography,* January 1980

[3]*Rolling Stone,* April 7, 1977, p. 49

[4]*Circus,* September 13, 1976, p. 42

Chapter 6

"Let's Get Physical"

Sex has always been a seller on TV as well as on the radio, but in recent years even so-called pop singers have begun to use sex as their seller.

Olivia Newton-John, who had been looked on for years as a clean pop singer, set pornography to music with her recent hit "Physical." A segment of the song says, "I took you to an intimate restaurant, then to a suggestive movie. There's nothing left to talk about unless it's horizontal (laying down). Let's get physical, physical. I want to hear your body talk."

Another verse says, "I'm sure you understand my point of view. We know each other mentally. You gotta know that you're bringin' out the animal in me. Let's get physical, physical; I wanna hear your body talk."

With lyrics like this it's no wonder that a recent Norman-Harris survey found that almost one out of three 13-to 15-year-olds and six out of ten 16- to 18-year-olds have experienced sexual intercourse.

Last year in America alone there were over 275 thousand abortions among teenagers. Many rock stars openly promote their views on sex which include perversions of every kind.

The manager of the group *Aerosmith* explains, "When you're in a certain frame of mind, particularly sexually oriented, there's nothing better than rock and roll."[1]

John Lennon of the *Beatles* described the tours the *Beatles* took as complete orgies, explaining how the group was followed by whores.[2]

Robin Gibbs of the *Bee Gees* confesses to the hobby of pornographic drawing.[3]

Daryl Hall of *Hall & Oates* says, "The idea of having sex with a man doesn't turn me off. I had lots of strange experiences with older boys between when I was four and fourteen."[4]

David Bowie was the first pop star to openly proclaim his homosexuality.[6] He and his wife met while they were both involved with the same man. Alice Cooper has a song entitled "I Love the Dead." It is an anthem to necrophilia.

His hits include "Cold Ethyl," "Only Women Bleed," and "Working Up a Sweat" which is a song about working up a sweat during the act of sex.

Elton John's song "Sweet Pointed Lady" is about the "virtue" of prostitution. He's been quoted as saying, "There's nothing wrong with going to bed with somebody of your own sex. I think people should be very free with sex. . . ."[7]

Of all these who thrive on sex-centered songs, the one who sticks out the most is Rod Stewart, with songs like "Tonight's the Night," "Hot Legs" and his latest hit "Tonight I'm Yours." Stewart comes prancing out on stage in his tight, leopard-skin pants which, in one of his recent tours, ripped in the middle of the concert. He openly proclaimed, in an interview with the *Rolling Stone Magazine,* "I always wanted to be attractive to men. That's half the people who buy our records."[8]

For those of you who are accustomed to rock and roll, the above comes with little surprise. But to those who are not familiar with Janis Joplin, Alice Cooper and Rod Stewart, I'm sure you will agree that pornography has been set to music.

Richard Oldham (recording manager for the *Rolling Stones*) said, "Rock music is sex and you have to hit them (teenagers) in the face with it."[9]

Debbie Harry, former Playboy Bunny of the group *Blondie* says, "I've always thought that the main ingredients in rock are sex, a really good stage show and really sassy music. Sex and sass, I really think that's where it's at."[10]

In another interview she declared, "Rock and roll is all sex, 100 percent. Sometimes music can make you ————, what makes me ———— the most depends upon the person. I don't know if people ———— ——— to my music; I hope so. I wear tight clothes, I wear sexy clothes, I wear short skirts, try to look hot. If someone's undressing me with their eyes, that's not an offense to me. If someone's a pig then that's horrible . . . but I don't think somebody looking at me and envisioning me without my clothes is going to hurt me."[11]

Again she says, "Sex appeal makes us happy, complete people and not robots. People think of sex as depraved but it's the best thing we've got. Sex appeal comes from a person, not a body, from the power of positive thinking."[12]

Chris Stein, lead guitarist of *Blondie,* agrees "Everybody takes it for granted rock and roll is synonymous with sex."[13]

Shocked? It's about time! This has been going on for almost 20 years.

When the *Beatles* were in Las Vegas in 1964, all four of them could have been arrested for statutory rape. They were involved with two 14-year-old girls in their bedroom all night.[14]

Knowing of these things it's not hard to understand

why one female fan got so sexually stimulated at a *Van Halen* concert that she ran on stage and literally pulled down David Lee Roth's pants![15]

In a recent interview Roth proclaimed about their provocative image, "*Van Halen* is not an act. We are the way we look. Playing rock and roll is our license to live out our wildest fantasies."[16] Roth also said, "Whatever your vice, whatever your sexual ideals, whatever somebody can do in the nine-to-five job I can do in rock and roll. When I'm on stage my basement faculties take over completely. We're giving our daily lives melodies, beats and titles."[17]

One young lady interviewed along with *Van Halen* was asked what she thought about the group. "What I think about *Van Halen,*" she said, "is that I enjoy the show very much and the rock and roll definitely all the way. It's hard core; makes you want to move; makes you want to groove; makes you do anything you want to. And for another thing," she adds, smiling broadly at Roth, "every one of the guys in this band knows how to get down. That's for sure!"

After spending several days with *Van Halen* an interviewer said, "I've seen enough nude women and heard enough morning after anecdotes to fuel an article about Porn-rock!"

Roth later said, "As for me personally I feel sexy a whole lot of the time. That's one of the reasons I'm in this job is to exercise my sexual fantasies when I'm on stage."

Is it only sex that sells? One record promoter comments, "The kids with the clean songs are having a hard time coming up with hit songs."[18]

I am not naive enough to think that the only reason there is a sexual explosion is because of rock and roll, but I am equally not so stupid as to realize that rock is the heartbeat of teenagers today and that most teenagers would rather cut off their right arms than give up their rock music.

I've found that many young people are uncomfortable with the sexual pressure created by rock and roll and they

Top: Hall 'N Oates **often impersonate women and attempt to come across to their audiences as women. Hall reportedly is into witchcraft and a follower of Aleister Crowley.** ***Bottom:*** **Elton John admits he is bisexual and also into the occult.**

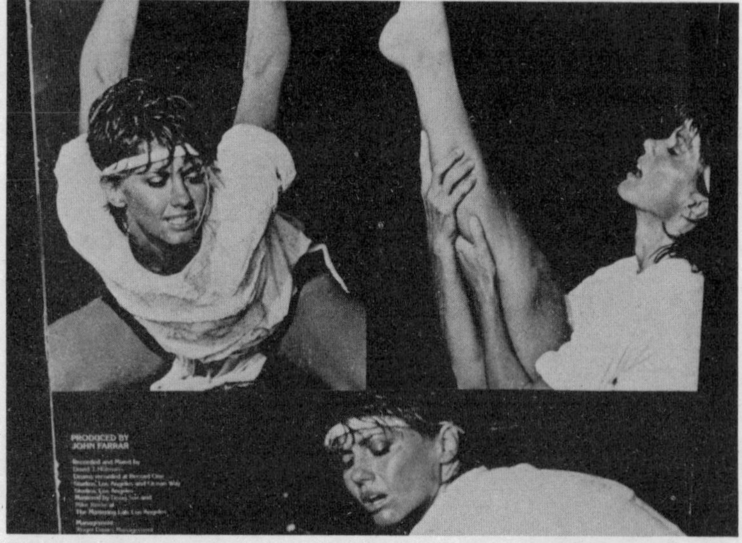

Top: Rod Stewart is one of the raunchiest of the rock and rollers and often performs songs with strong sexual overtones. *Bottom:* This album cover depicts Olivia Newton-John in her "Let's Get Physical" hit. During an interview she said she was exercising for the cover. The words of the song sing a different tune!

feel like they have to give in to be accepted by their peers.

There are honest answers for their questions about their discomfort.

One such youth was a 16-year-old I had been counseling for several months. She had a history of heavy drug involvement. One morning when I went to counsel her she came in acting rather timid, as though she knew I would not approve what she had done. After some brief small talk she revealed that she'd spent the night with her boyfriend and wanted me to tell her something to help her feel better about herself. But all I could do was tell her the truth: that she was used. And only by realizing this and asking Jesus to forgive her and cleanse her could she start anew.

God only does business with those who mean business. Any dead fish can float downstream with the rest; it takes live fish to swim upstream.

"Let's get physical" is one of the strong central themes of rock. If you don't believe me, maybe you'll believe yet another authority in the music business. "Don't forget the ——— is mightier than the sword,"[20] says screamin' Jay Hawkins, a forerunner on the rock and roll scene. Or perhaps this one: "Rock and roll meant ——— (sexual intercourse) originally, which I don't think is a bad idea. Let's bring it back again," said Waylon Jennings.[21]

All these are old timers from the rock scene, but what concerns me more are those like one 14-year-old who wrote to one rock editor, "Rock and sex mix like rum and coke."

[1]*Rolling Stone,* December 2, 1970, p. 35

[2]*Rolling Stone,* January 7, 1971, p. 34

[3]*Rolling Stone,* May 17, 1977

[4]*Rolling Stone,* April 21, 1977, p. 15

[5]*People Magazine,* August 18, 1975, p. 68

[6]*Rolling Stone,* October 7, 1976, p. 17

[7]*Rolling Stone,* June 21, 1973, p. 39

[8]*Time,* April 28, 1967, p. 72

[9]*Hit Parade,* September 1979, p. 31
[10]*Circus,* July 7, 1977, p. 40
[11]*People Magazine,* March 16, 1981, p. 88
[12]*People Magazine,* May 21, 1979
[13]*Parade,* October 4, 1964, p. 12
[14]*Rockline,* Spring, 1981, p. 30
[15]*Circus,* July 31, 1982, p. 32
[16]*Time,* July 1, 1966, p. 57
[17]*Time,* July 1, 1966, p. 57
[18]*The Book of Rock Lists,* p. 8
[19]*The Book of Rock Lists,* p. 8
[20]*Hard Rock,* June 1978

Chapter 7

Rock and Roll Tombstones

Many rock stars take drugs, following all the others who have gone before them on the path to self-destruction. This road is paved with tombstones of both men and women who once had the world in the palm of their hands as they sang and played the tunes of songs that shook the world.

It would seem that most of these followed the 10th commandment of rock and roll given by Robert Hunter, long-time lyricist for the *Grateful Dead.* "Destroy yourself," he said, "physically and mentally, and insist that all true brothers do likewise as an expression of unity."[1]

In a kindred spirit, rock star Pete Townsend said, "Pop (or rock) has become solemn, irrelevant and boring. What it needs now is more noise, more size, more sex, more violence, more gimmickery, more vulgarity. And, above all, it definitely needs a new messiah who will take things back to the glamour, power and insanity of the Elvis Presley age."[2]

He was also quoted as saying, "Rock and roll is all that counts."[3]

Perhaps those who died were in the process of becoming the new rock and roll messiahs.

But to be a messiah one must not only be able to save himself, but also bring salvation to others. A messiah must be able to control all circumstances, be all-knowing, all powerful, and everywhere at once.

When we look at these factors we see why these rock idols are dead today, for they attempted to be supernatural beings through their natural bodies. And, as all good captains who realize the ship is sinking, they went down with it. Attempting to be everything to everyone, they turned to various substances hoping to find the power and strength they needed.

For the following, the substance of their strength became the substance of their death.

Death from drug overdose or similar circumstances:[4]

1) Tommy Bolin, (*Deep Purple; James Gang*) 1950-75
2) Tim Buckley, 1947-75
3) Nick Drake, 1948-74
4) Tim Harpen, 1940-80
5) Jimi Hendrix, 1942-70
6) Gregory Harbert (*Blood, Sweat & Tears*) 1950-78
7) Janis Joplin, 1943-70
8) Frankie Lymon, 1942-68
9) Robbi McIntosh (*Average, White Band*) 1944-74
10) Keith Moon, 1946-78
11) Gram Parsons, 1946-73
12) Elvis Presley, 1935-77
13) Sid Vicious (*The Sex Pistols*) 1958-79
14) Danny Whitten (*Crazy Horse*) 1945-72
15) Alan Wilson (*Canned Heat*) 1943-70
*16) John Boham (*Led Zeppelin*) 1945-80

**Alcohol related resulting in suffocation from vomit.*

Suicides

1) Johnny Ace, 1929-54
2) Ian Curtis *(Joy Division)*
3) Pete Ham *(Bad Finger)* 1947-75
4) Donny Hathaway, 1945-79
5) Phil Ochs, 1940-76
6) Rory Storm, 1941-74
7) Paul Williams *(Temptations)* 1939-73

The only names that have been omitted from the categories above are those who followed in the steps of these many stars. Those who were your friends, cousins, brothers, and even sons and daughters!

The above are just a few more than were trampled to death at a recent *Who* concert in Cincinnati. Eleven young people were crushed when they were trapped inside a crowd surging to get inside the coliseum. One California T-shirt marketer is now selling T-shirts that say, "I'd walk over you to see *The Who.*" Such humor shows just how far away some have strayed from holding any principles about anything at all.

The losers of the life-style and philosophies preached through rock are not only those who have died, but those of us who live in a society brainwashed with a new morality ideology.

Even the legendary Mick Jagger of the *Rolling Stones* has said, "Too many people are obsessed with pop music. The position of rock and roll in our subculture has become far too important, especially in delving for philosophical content."

As long as these rock stars are looked upon as the messiahs of our age there will be those who live through their tunes, only to wind up in tombs.

[1] *Book of Rock Lists,* by Dave Marsh and Kevin Stein, p. 5
[2] *Book of Rock Lists,* p. 6
[3] *Book of Rock Lists,* p. 5
[4] *Book of Rock Lists,* p. 459
[5] *Book of Rock Lists,* p. 7

Chapter 8

Drugs, Drink and Rock and Roll

Drugs and rock and roll have gone together down through the years. To think otherwise is like thinking of Alaska without snow!

One rock manager stated, "No matter what anyone tells you, drugs will always be a part of the rock scene."[1]

I believe it all started becoming evident when the *Beatles* began singing songs like "I Get High With a Little Help From My Friends," "Fixing a Hole," and "Lucy in the Sky With Diamonds" (LSD).

Time Magazine reviewed one of their albums called *Sergeant Pepper's Lonely Hearts Club Band* and said it was literally drenched in drugs![2]

John Lennon admitted to having been on pills since he was seventeen. He also admitted their rooms were always "full of dope."

During a series of interviews in early 1971, Lennon said that he and Yoko Ono had taken heroin and that all four of the *Beatles* took LSD. Of himself he said, "I must have had a thousand trips. I used to eat it all the time."[3]

Janie Villiers, who lived for one year with the *Rolling Stones,* said in a magazine interview, "Another thing that took some getting used to was the rolled-up $20-and $50-dollar bills I would find stuffed in the sofa.[4]

"I was a bit naive at the time. Rose had to tell me they were used to snort cocaine. I also had been finding little piles of what looked like talc, and I would promptly vacuum them up. When Rose caught me doing this she said, 'Janie, we like you very much, but you're costing us a great deal of money. You just sucked up about a gram of cocaine into the Hoover!' "

Another who is outspoken about the period during which he lived with the *Rolling Stones* is Tony Sanchez. As he reports in his book he was Keith Richards' primary drug connection, often spending $1,000 daily on exotic drugs for Keith and his entourage.[5]

When Tony was asked how Anita Pallenburg (Keith's mistress) reacted to his book he replied, "If looks could kill I'd be dead. I don't think she will ever forgive me. That really scares me because I'm afraid of her because she is an evil woman. All of that stuff about Anita and witchcraft in the book is true. I have seen it work. . . . The day my book was published I had to go to the hospital and have my stomach cut open because I was in terrible pain and I really believe it was one of her spells. The doctors found nothing!"

On February 12, 1967, Keith Richards, Mick Jagger and Marianne Faithful were busted at Richards' home in the Redlands, West Wittering, U.K., known as the "celebrated drug orgy raid!"[6]

The home of George and Patty Harrison of the *Beatles* was raided on March 12, 1969. One hundred and twenty joints (marijuana cigarettes) were found.[7]

In Tokyo, on January 16, 1980, customs inspectors discovered nearly a half pound of marijuana that Paul McCartney had absent-mindedly left in his suitcase.[8]

The *Grateful Dead* bassist, Pet Lesh, was busted for possession of drugs in Martin County, California, on January 14, 1973.[9]

Thirty-three-year-old rock star Ron Henley, of the *Eagles,* was fined $2,500 and put on two year's probation after pleading no contest to a charge of giving drugs to a sixteen-year-old girl found nude in his home last fall. He was sentenced in Santa Monica, California, on the misdemeanor charge of contributing to the delinquency of a minor.[10]

Glen Fry of the *Eagles* said, "I'm in the music business for sex and narcotics."[11]

Fleetwood Mac bassist John McVie was fined $1,000 after pleading guilty in the Wailuku Circuit Court in Hawaii on March 9. The charges were three counts of failing to register firearms, but cocaine possession charges against McVie were dropped.[12]

Julie Ann, his American wife, pleaded guilty to charges of promoting a dangerous drug (cocaine) and "hindering prosecution by attempting to flush the cocaine down the toilet." After intercepting a package containing 4.5 grams of cocaine (and removing 3.5 grams of it), police tracked the parcel to McVie's big wooden house in the Napali resort area of the Island of Maui in Hawaii on December 23.

Lead singer of the group *Aerosmith* boasts of his drug arrest while in the 11th grade and also about when police busted 52 young people at one of their concerts. Aerosmith paid $3,650 to bail out the drug offenders.[13]

The *Bee Gees* say they avoid all hard drugs, such as cocaine, but do smoke marijuana every now and then.[14]

David Bowie has confessed to a deep involvement in drugs from heroin to cocaine. He admits, "Actually I was junked out of my mind . . . you can do good things with drugs, but then comes the long decline."[15]

Members of the group *Jefferson Starship* were repeatedly arrested for drug usage. Lead guitarist Paul Kanter com-

Top: **Debbie Harry of the group *Blondie* talks openly of sexual perversions during interviews. *Bottom:* The *Rolling Stones* dressed up like witches for this album entitled *Satanic Majesties Request.***

mented, "The group paid for it (the drugs) as if it were a business expense."[16]

Grace Slick of the group is called by many "the Acid Queen of Rock and Roll." Motherhood did slow down her dropping somewhat.

"It's hard to keep an eye on the kid when you're hallucinating,"[17] Ritchie Blackmore said in a recent interview, "I'm usually very drunk when I play. Part of me is shy and I have to drink to come out of myself."[18]

With stars like these representing success to the young people of our generation, it is no wonder that a recent Norman-Harris pole showed the following report on teenagers: 53 percent of 13- to-15-year-olds and 78 percent of the 16-to-18-year-olds drink whiskey, beer or wine occasionally. Almost 75 percent of the high schoolers say they have tried marijuana; nearly half experimented with it by the time they were 15![19]

"It's not the 'in' thing anymore," explained one 14-year-old. "It's just part of everybody's life!"

While most of the teenagers think their parents know they drink, only three out of ten believe their parents know they smoke marijuana.

Too many parents are quick to say, "Not my teenager!"

I recently counseled a young high school girl who had a reputation at school as an alcoholic, but her parents assured me that she was the model teenager who didn't talk back, kept her room clean and did all she was told. It's just like so many young people have told me, "Sure my parents know I'm doing drugs. But they don't want to admit it to themselves, so they just ignore it and pretend it's not there."

Too many young people are adhering to the words of Jimi Hendrix who said, "Rock is so much fun. That's what it's all about; filling up the chest cavities (smoking dope) and the empty knee caps and elbows (shooting up)."[20]

[1]*Circus,* April 17, 1979, p. 16
[2]*Rolling Stone,* January 7, 1971
[3]*Time,* January 18, 1971
[4]*45,* March 17, 1981, p. 40-45
[5]*Circus,* December 11, 1979, p. 34-37
[6]*The Book of Rock Lists,* p. 480
[7]*The Book of Rock Lists,* p. 480
[8]*The Book of Rock Lists,* p. 482
[9]*The Book of Rock Lists,* p. 482
[10]*Minneapolis Tribune,* February 26, 1981, p. 3a
[11]*People,* June 30, 1975, p. 30
[12]*Rolling Stone,* April 16, 1981, p. 87
[13]*Rolling Stone,* December 2, 1970, p. 35
[14]*Circus,* August 3, 1973, p. 38
[15]*Rolling Stone,* January 12, 1978, p. 13
[16]*Rolling Stone,* September 30, 1971, p. 30
[17]*Newsweek,* February 8, 1971
[18]*Circus,* May 31, 1982, p. 30
[19]*McCalls,* October 1981, p. 30
[20]*The Book of Rock Lists,* p. 8

Chapter 9

Rock: The Church of Today

If you have very many teenage friends, are a teenager yourself, or are one of those who has raised teenagers, then I'm sure you have heard this conversation before.

"He just won't go to church. I don't know why! He came in late Saturday night after being out with his friends and we went in to wake him up the next morning and he said he didn't want to go. His father and I talked and we decided we'd better not force him."

This conversation is typical of millions of parents who attend church and love God. I couldn't tell you how many parents have come to me and recited this same conversation you've just read. What many do not realize is that their teenagers haven't given up religion, but have simply joined a new one: the Religion of Rock and Roll.

I was once a member of it myself. Now if you would have asked me back then if this was true I would have denied it. But, in fact, everything that I believed could be found in the rhyming lyrics of rock and roll. If you find this hard to believe then just examine rock from its inception in the 50's.

In the 50's it brought a new way of dressing and a new way of talking.

In the 60's it brought in loose morals, a devastating lack of respect for authority, and drugs. It seemed as though the young people of America had eaten, injected or smoked every fowl thing possible.

The mid-sixties to early seventies could best be described as the "if it feels good do it" decade. The rock influence began in America in the 50's, but the tidal wave came from Britain with the most powerful rock and roll evangelists. The religion of rock had begun.

Rock star Billy Squier put it this way in a recent interview, "The whole British music scene of the mid-sixties had a pretty profound effect on me. It started with the *Rolling Stones,* the *Who,* the *Kinks* and the *Beatles.* British rock and roll became the gospel for American kids like me."[1]

The interviewer goes on to say, "Now Billy Squier is taking the gospel to America and Europe, preaching his own rock sermons in sold-out concerts."

If you think Billy Squier is the only one who feels that way listen to what veteran rocker Leon Russell said in an interview, "I'd like to say that organized Christianity has done more harm than any other single force I can think of in the world."

When asked what the alternative would be he suggested, "The religion of rock and roll."[2]

Still surprised? You can see why rock has had such a devastating effect on America and the entire civilized world.

Pete Townsend of the *Who* said, "People say, you've gotta go on man, otherwise all those kids they'll be finished, they'll have nothing to live for, that's rock and roll."[3]

Alan Freed, the man who named rock, said, "Let's face it, rock and roll is bigger than all of us."[4]

Larry Williams said, "It has no beginning and no end,

for it is the very pulse of life itself!"[5]

You can't imagine how many young rockers I have challenged to stay away from their rock for just one week, just to hear the response, "Well if I wanted to I could."

I was speaking on rock at a major college campus and many students had come to hear what I had to say. The local college rock station had an outdoor rock show in protest of what I was speaking about.

One college student, upset with what I was saying, jumped up and said, "I could quit listening to rock and roll whenever I want." Another student, who agreed with what I was saying, jumped up and yelled, "Well then quit!" The first student's response was, "Well I don't want to!"

There still may be some of you who would think that to say rock is a religion in itself would be extreme. Let's examine the term religion. When someone joins a religion three things change with them.

1. Their philosophy
   (where they place their values and what they feel is important).

2. Their talk, slang words, phrases
   (most religions have their own jargon).

3. The outward appearance
   (wear what others in the religion wear, be it short hair, suits, turbans, caps, hats, etc.).

These same things change with devout rockers. The rock scene has its own set of values; it also has its own vocabulary. And, whether punk rock, new wave or heavy metal, they all have their own style of dress. Young people are blindly giving their lives to the values of the rock and roll religion.

One such young person I met while in California was 15 years old. She was a punk rocker who was brought to me for counseling. I will never forget when she walked into the room with her parents. She had enough eye make-up on to be a walking display for a make-up company.

I wondered how she kept her eyes open.

She sat down and began to tell me her story. Her parents wouldn't let her listen to her kind of music or let her hang around with her punk rock friends and they didn't like her punk rock clothing.

"If you were a mom and had a teenage daughter," I asked her, "that was wanting to live like you do, would you let her?"

"No," she whispered.

I called for someone to come in with a cosmetic mirror and let her look at her make-up piled on her face.

I asked, "Can you tell me what is attractive about what you have on?"

"No," she replied again.

You see the truth is she never really had taken a good look at herself. She wore what everyone else wore because that was her way of being a part of the rock scene.

The rock stars of today are not ignorant to the standards they create by their own life-styles.

One such rock star is Ozzy Osbourne, former lead singer for *Black Sabbath,* and presently leading his own group.

Ozzy said in a recent interview, "No matter what you do, you've always got to admit that there are certain minority groups in America that always want to screw things up for other people; always want to stop people from enjoying themselves. And the thing is they can't because rock and roll is a religion itself."

Guitarist Craig Chaquico of *Jefferson Starship* said, "Rock concerts are the churches of today. Music puts them on a spiritual plane. All music is God."

With statements like this you can see why many rock fans now are wearing shirts that say, "________ is God." Whatever the name of their favorite group is, that's who they consider as their god.

Listen to Webster's definition of a god. "(1) Any of various beings conceived of as supernatural and immortal, a male deity, (2) an idol, (3) a person or thing deified, the Creator and ruler of the universe, supreme being."

Can you see why one teenage fan wrote *Rolling Stone Magazine* after the death of Jimi Hendrix and said, "Oh God, I can't make it without Jimi. I can't, I can't."

Whether you would like to believe it or not, music is becoming more spiritual than ever before and many rock stars are demanding nothing less than worship. That is why there is such devout anti-establishment movements like *Punk Rock,* where the norm is to turn your back on everything that is considered normal. It is a total change of life just like conversion.

Whatever you turn to for enjoyment and peace, whatever you think the most about, whatever you spend most of your extra money on: That is your god!

[1]*Circus,* July 31, 1982, p. 47

[2]*Rolling Stone,* December 2, 1970, p. 35

[3]*The Book of Rock Lists,* p. 95

[4]*The Book of Rock Lists,* p. 8

[5]*The Book of Rock Lists,* p. 8

Chapter 10

Cults

With all the occultic influence in rock it would hardly seem there would be room for cults but there is.

In the mid-sixties it became a popular thing to be involved with some sort of cult. The popularity has somewhat worn off, but the effects of that time period haven't.

Young people on college campuses became easy game and fresh blood for every Eastern thought and California dream. It seemed as though the drug culture needed something to believe in.

So Hindus and gurus began to pop up everywhere. The following are the past and present religious persuasions of rock stars:

George Harrison, Krishna[1]

Hare Krishna originated in India with a Hindu sect led by Lord Chaitanya. Krishna is one of the many gods in the

Hindu myths. Thousands of Indians believe that a Hindu, born in 1865, was the promised reincarnation of a saint and the embodiment of the god Krishna. His name was Sri Haranath and he died in May of 1927.

Abhay Charan De Bhaktivedanta Swam Prabhupada, a businessman for 30 years in India, believed he was chosen to preach the Krishna message in English.

He arrived in New York in 1965 and began his work in Greenwich Village by public chantings.

George Harrison's song "My Sweet Lord" was dedicated to Lord Krishna. Background vocals on the song are "Hare, Hare, Hare Krishna."

Transcendental Meditation (TM)

The following are performers connected with Maharishi Mahesh Yogi, founder of TM:[2]

The Beach Boys
The Beatles
Mia Farrow
Donovan
Paul Horn
Marianne Faithful
Mick Jagger *(Rolling Stones)*
Brian Jones *(Rolling Stones)*
Robbie Krieger (The *Doors)*
Ray Manzarek (The *Doors)*
Skip Spence *(Moby Grape)*
Maurice White *(Earth, Wind, and Fire)*
Verdine White *(Earth, Wind and Fire)*

Maharishi Mahesh Yogi founded TM in Calfornia in 1959. He was formerly a pupil of Guru Dev, who was a leader of a Hindu sect in India. Although claiming to be non-religious, this group is undoubtedly basically Hindu. They believe that the purpose of life is happiness sought through an endless cycle of incarnations and reincarnations. God is an impersonal "Creative Intelligence."

"Seeking to discover who we are" transforms them into "bliss consciousness" and it is only attained through the seven steps of Transcendental Meditation, they believe. This is accomplished by reciting endlessly a liturgy called the *Mantra*. The *Mantras* represent chants to Hindu deities. TM estimates assets of $200 million.[3]

Seals and Crofts "Bahaism"[4]

Far more popular than many eastern-based religions is a religion coming out of Iran: Bahai.

Mirza Ali Mohammed was the son of a Persian merchant. On May 23, 1844, he claimed to be a manifestation (or public evidence) of God on earth. He gave himself the title of *Bab*. This is Arabic for "gate." He predicted that an even greater deliverer would appear and this new deliverer would usher in the dawn of a new age. The new greater deliverer (following after Bab) was to be the Baha-ullah (splendor of God). Bahai takes its name from Baha-ullah. Bahais are those who accept Baha-ullah as the "demonstration of God" for this age.

Carlos Santana: Sri Chinmoy

Sri Chinmoy is a guru who has various teachings. Carlos Santana, leader of the group *Santana*, is a devout disciple of his. In one interview, Carlos said he planned to survive more deeply to his guru in the future.[5]

Jehovah's Witness

The following names are those who are or were associated with the Jehovah's Witness:

Lester Bangs
George Benson
Ornette Coleman
Larry Graham *(Sly and the Family Stone)*
Hank Markin *(The Shadows)*
Van Morrison
Hugh "Piano" Smith
David Thomas *(Pere Ubu)*

[1]*Satan's Angels Exposed,* Salem Kirban, p. 277

[2]*The Book of Rock Lists,* Dave Marsh & Kevin Stein, p. 418

[3]*Satan's Angels Exposed,* p. 281

[4]*Satan's Angels Exposed,* p. 102

[5]*Circus,* July 6, 1976, p. 45

[6]*The Book of Rock Lists,* p. 417

Chapter 11

Who's a Rock Rebel?

"OK, I'll give up most of my music, but not the *Beatles*. They're my favorite group!"

This is a typical statement. I hear it from today's teenagers and adults alike.

In response I share a story with them and I would like to share it with you.

This story is found in a book of the Bible. God told a man named Saul to go and wipe out a group of people called the Amalekites. He was instructed to kill everything in their camp, including animals.

At one time God's people had to cross through the land of the Amalekites and, as they were going through the land, the Amalekites would wait for the last people to cross over. Then they would jump them. The last people in line were usually the pregnant woman and old people. The Amalekites would take swords and rip unborn children out of their mothers' wombs.

So God remembered what they had done to his people

and told Saul, in I Samuel 15, to take the army and destroy them all. So Saul, being ruler over the Israelites at the time, did as God instructed him except that he saved the best animals and the Amalekite king.

God was displeased that Saul didn't follow his instructions.

Samuel was a prophet that God spoke through in those days. God told Samuel to go and tell Saul that he had disobeyed God.

When Samuel caught up with Saul and asked him why he had disobeyed God, Saul denied that he had.

Then Samuel said, "If you obeyed the commandment of the Lord, then what are all those fat cows and sheep doing out here with you? Where did they come from?"

And Saul said, "The people kept them; but all the bad things we totally destroyed."

Then Samuel replied, "Why didn't you obey God? When you were little in your own eyes you obeyed God! God told you to go and destroy everything of the Amalekites, but you have disobeyed and done evil in the sight of God."

Again Saul denied this and said that he intended to use the animals to offer a sacrifice to God.

But Samuel told him, "God has more delight in your obedience than he does in your sacrifices or burnt offerings. For rebellion (not complete obedience) is as the sin of witchcraft and stubbornness is as the sin of idolatry (worshipping things other than God). Because you have rejected what God told you Saul, God has rejected you from being King."

So Saul was no longer king and God placed David in his place.

The worst part is yet to come.

At about that time the Philistines came and started to fight God's people. So Saul went out to fight them, even though God was no longer with him. During the battle Saul was wounded and, instead of letting the enemy kill him, he pulled out his sword and fell on it. But it didn't kill him. II Samuel 1:8 tells us that an Amalekite came walking by and killed Saul. There wouldn't have been an Amalekite alive to kill him had he obeyed God.

The same principle applies to anything that God tells you to get rid of in your own life. If you don't kill it, then it will kill you, as with Saul. There are seven things to check for, in your own life, to see if you are a rebel against God:

1. Rebels never do all of what they're told to do.
2. They're never completely honest with themselves or with others.
3. They are "blameshifters," always placing the blame on others and not themselves.
4. They will give up wrongs but not their rights. As with Saul they will give up the bad and keep what they feel is good.
5. They are always questioning the authority of others, "Who are you to tell me what is right or wrong?" As with Saul who denied Samuel's accusation.
6. They are very prideful, thinking highly about themselves. Saul was like that.
7. They are very stubborn with the "I'm right and you're wrong" attitude, instead of being humble and examining the facts to see if they be true.

Previously in the story Saul resorted to witchcraft because God was no longer leading him in his decisions.

Because they are in rebellion, rock groups also seek their answers through witchcraft!

Alice Cooper was fully aware of what he was saying when he stated, "Rebellion is the basis for our group."

Jim Steinman of *Meat Loaf* said, "We've always been fascinated by the supernatural and have always felt that rock was the perfect idiom for it."[1]

The lead singer for *Meat Loaf* adds, "When I go on stage I become possessed."[2]

Sting, a member of the new rock sensation called *Police* said, "We'll probably get into drugs and Eastern mysticism (occult) to get our songs. In fact," he adds, "some of us already are."[3]

While traveling in the United States, Europe and, occasionally, in the Philippine Islands, I have taken a poll among teenagers.

"When you get into an argument with your parents," I asked, "how many of you go into your room and turn on your rock and roll?" Fifty to 75 percent of the teens polled said yes. Rebellion loves company.

Here are six steps that lead to rebellion:

1. Disobedience
2. Self-deceit (not honest with yourself)
3. Stubbornness
4. Looking for idols
5. Witchcraft and the occult
6. Death

If you see any of these steps in your life, or in the lives of those around you, it's not too late to stop the pattern. You don't have to live the life of a "rock and roll rebel."

CAUTION: The end of rebellion is always death.

[1] *Circus*, December 22, 1977, p. 12

[2] *Time*, September 11, 1978

[3] *Creem*, July-August, 1982

Chapter 12

Not My Group

I remember the first time I spoke on the subject of rock and roll. Little did I realize the impact it was going to have on the community of Waco, Texas. My one-week engagement turned into three weeks.

After I spoke the first night we decided to have everyone bring in the records that they wanted to get rid of and the following evening we would burn them.

When I walked outside to where the records were to be burned and saw how many there were, I was amazed. I was not the only one surprised. So were the newspaper reporters and television crewman who were sent to cover the story.

Even before the burning the church started receiving obscene phone calls. And the first container we were going to use to burn them was stolen by a group of teenagers. Every few minutes during the burning a carload of teenagers would drive by swearing, cursing and screaming out, "Rock is here to stay. It will never die!"

Local rock stations said we were afraid to upset the local country-western fans, so we picked on rock.

There were also students from a local religious college who were arguing over what's wrong with rock music and the questionable value of burning the records.

There were some people who wouldn't give up certain albums if I didn't have concrete evidence that the group was involved in the occult. I couldn't understand how people refused to see the sexual and occultic overtones in rock.

But I found the real problem with rock came out in my conversation with a girl stuck on the group *Journey*.

"So what if I'm not giving up *Journey*," she said.

I made her angry when I asked her if she knew what an idol is.

"It's something that comes between you and God," I explained, "something that you won't give up. And anything you can't give up . . . well, you don't have it but it has you! Jesus said either you are for me or against me."

Music was created by God to glorify him. Any music that does not glorify God is a perversion of what God intended. If people are using music for their own purposes, then they've stolen God's gift and are using it selfishly.

The question is not whether the group is sexually perverted, immoral or even in the occult. If you are a Christian, then every record you buy from a secular group is helping them financially. If the group is into drugs, then you support their drug habits by purchasing their albums. If they buy sex then you're supporting that.

"But," some of you may say, "I don't buy records. I just listen to the radio." Sorry, but if you listen to them on the radio, you are still supporting them.

Radio stations make their money from advertisers who purchase air time to advertise products. The way they get advertisers to buy time is by a listening rating taken through polls. The higher the listening audience the more advertisement time that station will be able to sell. When an advertiser sees that a station carries a large type and age audience they're trying to reach, then they'll buy time. This causes the radio station to continue playing particular groups and certain types of music. In understanding this you can see how important it is what station you listen to.

There have been so many young people who have left my meetings and, for the first time, have really seen the real message of rock.

There have also been many who left and said I was crazy and that they would never give up rock whether it was satanic or not.

I don't know where you stand, but I do ask you to consider the words of Jesus, "No man can serve two masters. Either he will cling to the one and hate the other or hate the one and cling to the other."

What about your favorite group?

1. Do they glorify God?
2. Are they building God's kingdom or destroying it?
3. Can you see Jesus is Lord in their lives?
4. Are they serving themselves or the Living God?

"But if I give up my rock what can I listen to?" you may ask.

Today more than ever before Christians have an alternative to non-Christian music. One of the greatest things that has happened in the Christian world today is many "rock and rollers" have turned to Christ and he has changed both their music and their message.

Putting it in the words of an English friend of mine, "Christ has put their feet on the Rock and their names on the roll!"

Unfortunately many Christian artists are suffering financially because Christians are supporting non-Christian artists.

Former lead singer of the group *Santana,* Leon Patillo, has turned to Christ. His new music is better than ever. His songs are scripturally sound and bring you into the presence of God.

Barry McGuire, also a former rock star, now sings songs filled with the life of God. Barry's honesty in what he sings and shares is without comparison.

Formerly of the *New Christy Minstrels,* Barry sang the top ten protest hit "Eve of Destruction." Now he sings of the King of Life.

Keith Green was also one who wrote for secular records, but changed his tune. Keith's music and message, before his recent death, brought thousands to Christ. I am sure his music will continue to do the same.

One Swedish Christian girl said, "Keith Green's music says more than any other American I have heard."

There are no more excuses why Christian young people cannot hear good quality music about the "Rock that never rolls" . . . Jesus Christ.

Chapter 13

Stairway to Heaven?

Crowned by a popular rock magazine as "the most popular band in the world," *Led Zeppelin* is known for swinging concert tours as well as their music.

Their album *Led Zeppelin IV* was named the best album of the seventies along with their "Stairway to Heaven" as the best song.[1]

But their actions would cause many of us to question their popularity. In one Hollywood Hotel they destroyed a painting, submerged four stereos into bathtubs and ran motorcycle races in the hallways.

Other tales include one rock magazine's account of a groupie they doused with a bucket of urine.

Lead singer Robert Plant admits to having a fascination with Black Magic and refuses to visit the Boleskine Home (Page's mansion, formerly owned by the late Aleister Crowley).[2]

Guitarist of the group, Jimmy Page, owned his own occult book store at one time. He was quoted as saying,

"There was not one good collection of books on the occult in London, and I was tired of having to go to different places to get the books I wanted."[3]

A recent string of tragedies in the life of Page and other members of the group have led many to believe that he is reaping what he has sown.

When the album cover of *Stairway to Heaven* is opened up, the first thing you see is an old man holding a lantern. He is known as the Hermit in tarot cards. At the bottom you will see a little girl climbing a mountain in an attempt to reach the Hermit standing at the top with the lantern.

The Hermit of the tarot cards represents wisdom from above, silent council, prudence, an encounter with one who will guide you to material or spiritual goals. His lantern is a six-pointed star which represents the philosophy "Where I am there you also may be."[4]

Every practice in occult training aims at the union of personal consciousness with the cosmic will, which is the cause of all manifestations. With this information we understand the cover to be conveying that the occult is the stairway to heaven.

The title cut by the same name says, "Yes, there are two paths you can go by, but in the long run there's still time to change the road you're on and it makes me wonder." That same segment played backwards says, "There's no escaping it. It's my sweet Satan. The one will be the path who makes me sad; whose power is Satan."

In another segment of the song they sing, "Dear lady can you hear the wind blow and did you know that your stairway lies in the whispering wind?" Played backwards it says, "Oh I will sing because I live with Satan."

I'm sure that by now you are beginning to see the picture clearly. I'll let you be the judge of whether *Led Zeppelin* is really on the stairway to heaven!

I have spoken to many who are outraged to find the real message in "Stairway to Heaven."

I will never forget the man who shared with me an

obsession to hear the song at least once a day. I also must plead guilty of being a one-time lover of the song myself. I was unaware and shocked by the song's occultic meaning as many of you are.

Led Zeppelin is on no stairway to heaven but rather, if you pardon the expression, on the HIGHWAY TO HELL!

But one verse of the song is very true, "Yes there are two paths you can go by, but in the long run there's still time to change the road you're on." If you like the title "Stairway to Heaven," but are disappointed with the real meaning, there is a real stairway to heaven — through the cross of Jesus Christ.

[1]*Creem,* Winter, 1980 P. introduction (special edition)

[2]*Hit Parade,* July 1982, p. 7

[3]*Hit Parade,* July 1975, p. 64

[4]*The Tarot Revealed,* by Eden Gray, p. 168

Chapter 14 — Part I

Behind the Faces

AC/DC

AC/DC, easily one of the most popular heavy metal bands of the 80's, could rightfully describe their road to success in their 1979 LP titled *Highway to Hell.*

Bon Scott, 33-year-old lead singer for the group, died from asphyxiation, choking on his own vomit after an all night drinking binge. This incident, though tragic, didn't slow *AC/DC* down a bit.

"I thought, well . . . I'm not gonna sit around mopin' all year," guitarist Malcolm Young told *Rolling Stone.* "So I just rang up Angus Young (also of *AC/DC)* and said, 'Do you wanna come back and rehearse?' This was two days afterwards and I'm sure if it had been one of us Bon would have done the same thing" (*Rolling Stone,* December 25, 1980, p. 64).

Among their musical accomplishments are LP's *Back in Black, Highway to Hell, High Voltage, Let There Be Rock,* and the 1981 release of an album recorded five years earlier entitled *Dirty Deeds Done Cheap.* The nine songs on *Dirty Deeds* are trademark *AC/DC* themes (AC/DC means bisexual), says *Circus Magazine* writer Philip Bashe.

The titles of their songs leave the listener with no questions about *AC/DC's* moral stand.

The song "Squealer" represents *AC/DC* perfectly. This standard tale of sexual conquest concludes with a brag ("I've got the magic touch") but the song is so overdone that it's more like a cartoon than real life *(Circus,* June 30, 1981, p. 69). Other song titles include "Beating Around The Bush," "Love Hungry Man," and "The Jack," their ode to women inflicted with V.D.

Within ten weeks of its '81 release, "Dirty Deeds" streaked past the one million mark, reaching number three on the record charts. And if one song dominated FM radio in spring, 1981, it was the title track *(Circus,* December 31, 1981, p. 53).

Angus Young, member of *AC/DC,* said in a recent interview, "I rob banks, I rob people . . . mugging, raping, pillaging. I was born in Scotland, I'm 21 . . . but that varies. I started playing guitar when I was about 11. I'm generally lazy and I figured that this is the easiest way to make some money. This is what I do best. I saw all the women and I figured that looked good. . . . I got a guitar off my brother and I started playing anything" *(Hit Parader,* Fall 1982, p. 14).

It would seem that *AC/DC* has followed the lyrics of the song "Highway to Hell." ". . . Ain't nothin' I'd rather do, going down for the last time, my friends are gonna be there too, I'm on a highway to hell, on the highway to hell. Hey, Satan, paid my dues, playing in a rocking band. Hey momma, look at me, I'm on the way to the Promised Land, I'm on the highway to hell, I'm on the highway to hell. Don't stop me."

Adam and The Ants

Adam, leader of the group, has been thrust forth as a young hero. He represents rebellion, absurd fashion and bisexuality.

In a recent interview he said, "That's one of the most exciting things about pop music. When all the dressing up is taken aside, it revolves around sexuality. . . . When you go on (stage) there's a very sexual feeling . . . when they're (the fans) getting hot, sweaty, sticky and moving about. It's the closest thing to making love, really."

The same interview goes on to say, "So Adam remains a bit of an enigma, his shy androgyny attracting admirers of both sexes as he sings in 'The Magnificent Five': 'They believe in sex and looking good/with their own brand of music/they weren't pandering/so what side of the fence/are you on?' " *(Hit Parader,* Fall 1982, p. 40-41).

He ends up the interview saying, "I believe if there's any anarchy, let's make it sexual rather than political. Otherwise it's too scary . . . " *(Ibid,* p. 41).

Aerosmith

The main focus of the group is on the lead singer Steve Tyler.

Tyler's fantasies were fulfilled with Cyrinda Fox, whom he married after she became pregnant with his child.

Tyler boasts of his own arrest for drugs while in the 11th grade (Bob Larson *Rock).*

The manager of *Aerosmith* explains, "When you're in a certain frame of mind, particularly sexually oriented, there's nothing better than rock and roll" *(Rolling Stone,* December 2, 1970, p. 35).

He also was quoted as saying, "None of my groups will ever play Cincinnati again. The last time *Aerosmith* played Cincinnati somebody was shot." When asked about fans throwing things at him on stage Steve Tyler responded, "It's a manifestation of their excitement. They just get carried away. I wouldn't say it's a good manifestation, but it's hard to control" (*Circus,* May 4, 1980, p. 30-31).

Aerosmith's philosophy is seen clearly in their songs and can best be summed up in their song "Seasons of Wither" off the *Get Your Wings* LP. "Loose-hearted lady, sleepy was she. Love for the devil brought her to me; tears of a thousand drawn to her sin."

Allen Parsons Project

This group has an album called *Pyramid.* On the front cover there is a picture of pyramid power which causes an out-of-the-body experience.

The witchcraft overtones of pyramid power are carefully spelled out in the lyrics which say: "There are pyramids in my head. There's one under my bed. All you really need is a pyramid and just a little bit of luck I had read somewhere in a book and it's no lie, all you really need is a little bit of pyramidic help."

Allen Parsons Project also has an album entitled *Eve.* The album's front cover reveals two ladies' faces behind veils. If you take a close look you can see that both ladies have sores and warts on their faces.

One state's venereal disease investigator looked at the warts and sores on the faces in the picture and concluded that the ladies in the picture were suffering from secondary syphilis.

How many young people listening to *Eve* fully realize that the theme of the album is VD?

America

This group received national recognition and adulation with its first big hit "Horse With No Name" back in 1972.

During the next six years *America* became one of the hottest groups in America and cheering fans by the millions rushed out to hear their concerts. During a six-year period the group released eight gold albums, four of which sold so many records they earned the platinum rating.

America seemed to be in a dreamland — money, popularity, everything.

Then something went wrong. Their founder, Dan Peek, announced he was leaving the group.

"I looked back and thought to myself that I have everything I've always wanted," Peek said. "I'm rich but I soon came to realize that spiritually I was flat broke."

A short time later Peek turned his life over to Christ and was born again.

He continued to write songs but this time for the Lord.

However, when he took his songs to Warner Brothers, the company which had produced his first albums, they refused to consider his new works.

"Gee, Dan, you're a great artist and we would love to have you on the label but you just can't sing about Jesus," a Warner representative said.

That should tell us all a great deal about the rock and roll record industry. It's okay to cut records praising sexual immorality, sexual perversion, the occult and even about Satan worship — but not about Jesus!

Beach Boys

The *Beach Boys* were a 60's sensation that cashed in on their All-American look and California sound.

While millions of young American girls strolled beaches half clad in polkadot bikinis looking for the ultimate surfer boy, the *Beach Boys* sang their marching songs and lustful battle crys.

They have been deeply involved in Transcendental Meditation and even dedicated their *M.I.U.* album to

Maharishish International University.

They also have a song entitled "Transcendental Meditation."

Al Jardine, a member of the group, was asked: "Who do you think you were in a previous incarnation?"

Jardine answered, "We had our chart done once by Stephen Moffitt, our engineer, and it mentioned in there that Brian (another band member) and I were brothers in a past life and that Mike and I were also related in the past. But Brian and I came from such different backgrounds in this life! I came from the Midwest and Brian grew up in Hawthorne, California. Our only similarities are in music" (*Circus,* May 26, 1977, p. 51-52).

The *Beach Boys* were one of the first public groups to help launch TM and Maharishi Mahesh Yogi's occult teaching into the minds of the masses.

The Beatles

The *Beatles* are living legends. Their music brought with it a tidal wave of drugs, sex and the occult.

During a series of interviews in early 1971, Lennon admitted that he and Yoko Ono had taken heroin and that all four of the *Beatles* took LSD.

Of himself he said, "I must have had a thousand trips. I used to eat it all the time" (*Time,* January 18, 1971).

Time Magazine reviewed the *Sergeant Pepper's Lonely Hearts Club Band* LP and said it was "drenched in drugs."

John Lennon created an uproar by saying, "Christianity will go. We're more popular than Jesus now" (*Newsweek,* March 21, 1966).

In Lennon's book, *A Spaniard in the Works* (which is a blasphemy of Jesus), Lennon portrayed Christ as Jesus El Pifico, a garlic-eating, stinking little yellow, greasy fascist bastard catholic spaniard" (*A Spaniard in the Works,* Simon & Shuster, N.Y., p. 14).

While living in adultery, John and Yoko posed for nude photographs which provided the jacket for a *Beatle*-produced album entitled *The Two Virgins."*

"We don't believe in marriage but we thought we'd try it out," Lennon said. *(Parade,* April 27, 1969, p. 4).

The press officer for the *Beatles,* Derek Taylor, said, "They're completely anti-Christ. I mean, I am anti-Christ as well, but they're so anti-Christ they shock me which isn't an easy thing" *(Saturday Evening Post,* August 8, 1964).

Paul McCartney said, "We probably seem to be anti-religious because of the fact that none of us believe in God" *(Playboy,* February, 1965).

Ringo Starr said, "We are not anti-Christ, just anti-Pope and anti-Christian" *(Playboy,* February 1965).

George Harrison is a one-time follower of the Maharishi Mahesh Yogi. His song "My Sweet Lord" was dedicated to Hara Krishna. All the *Beatles* have been associated with TM (*The Book of Rock Lists,* Adell; Dave Marsh & Kevin Stein, p. 418).

After taking this behind-the-scenes look at the *Beatles* you can see why they would be anti-God and anti-Christ.

George Harrison was a leading backer behind the movie "The Life of Brian" (which was a mockery of Christ) (*Personality Parade,* Walter Scott, July 26, 1981, p. 2).

Paul McCartney was recently sued for a chunk of his $440 million fortune by his child born out of wedlock some 19 years ago in Hamburg, Germany *(People,* August 9, 1982, p. 24).

Bee Gees

While a first look at the *Bee Gees* would leave the impression that they are quite wholesome, a look into their private lives would expose the unwholesome values they have. The *Bee Gees* produced the biggest selling album of all times in the soundtrack to the movie "Saturday Night

Fever." The two-record set that featured five of the *Bee Gee's* original songs sold over 25 million copies.

Robin Gibb of the *Bee Gees* admits to a hobby of pornographic drawings and all three members (of the group) lace their comments with obscenities.

Barry insists that the album *Spirits Having Flown* is infiltrated with references to reincarnation, while Maurice and Robin lay claim to the psychic powers of ESP *(Rolling Stone,* May 17, 1979).

When asked about drugs, Barry Gibb said, "We avoid all hard drugs like cocaine, although we do smoke marijuana now and again . . ." *(Circus,* August 3, 1978, p. 36-38).

Black Sabbath

With a name like *Black Sabbath* you could only expect them to be what they are.

They were introduced to the British press by a party featuring the mock sword sacrifice of a semi-nude girl.

They were known to hold masses before some of their concerts. Their first album, *Black Sabbath,* pictured a witch on the front.

Another album *Sabbath Bloody Sabbath* shows a nude satanic ritual with the numbers 666 across the front of the album.

Albums like these make the message *Black Sabbath* is attempting to portray very clear.

A few months back I was watching *Black Sabbath* in concert on television. In the middle of the concert the lead singer of the band began to make a satanic salute. It is made by extending the little finger and the index finger. He yelled to the crowd and in response they also made the sign.

Then he looked at the sign he was making with his hand and said, "Some people think they know what this means

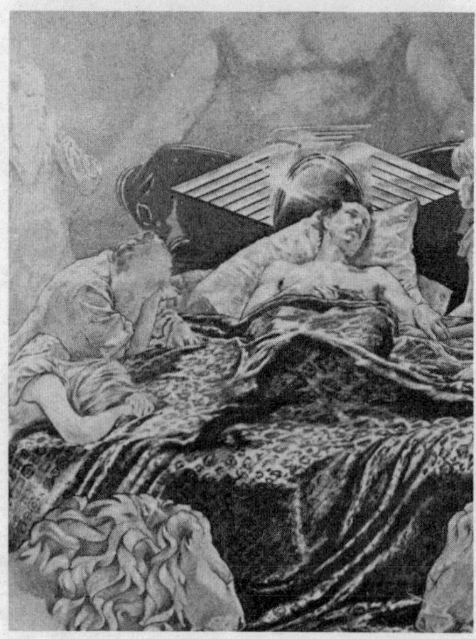

In the album *Sabbath Bloody Sabbath* the group *Black Sabbath* performs a nude satanic ritual. Note the mark of the beast, 666, in the top picture.

but we know what this really means. It means long live rock and roll.' "

The satanic salute can also be seen being made by Anton LaVey on the back of the "Satanic Bible."

Geezer Butler of the group claims that he is the seventh son of a seventh son, is Lucifer and can see the devil.

"It's a satanic world," admits Geezer, and he also believes in reincarnation (*Rolling Stone,* October 28, 1971, p. 41).

Bill Ward of the group admits that he feels "Satan could be God" (*Circus,* December 1971, p. 46).

Many groups feel a satanic overtone is appealing and sells. Such appeal, whether appealing to sell or not, is an open door for Satan to freely use. Don't forget: Satan uses every door open to him!

Blue Oyster Cult

B.O.C. is a group that has enjoyed a touch of the mystic and the occult.

The symbol that they use as their trademark, which is a cross with a question mark, can only be an anti-Christ symbol questioning what happened at the cross.

Their album *Agents of Fortune* shows a man holding tarot cards revealing "the one who comes against the power faces death." With his other hand he is pointing to their symbol; the cross with the question mark.

Other songs featured are "Hot Rails to Hell," "Harvester of the Eyes," "Sub-Human" and "Don't Fear the Reaper." The latter says "Don't be afraid of suicide."

Another of their songs, "E.T.I.," was dedicated to the belief in Extraterrestrial Intelligence.

Their album *Some Enchanted Evening* portrayed "death" riding on a horse.

Their newest album *Fire of Unknown Origin* shows people with different occultic symbols on their foreheads and

Top: **This album** ***Get Yourself Up*** **is a tribute to a truck-load of marijuana.** ***Bottom:*** **This album by the** ***Blue Oyster Cult*** **delves into tarot cards, witchcraft and the occult.**

clothes. The album is advertised by many rock magazines by saying "Follow the O-cult."

Ritchie Blackmore (of Rainbow)

Ritchie Blackmore, leader of the group *Rainbow,* was himself a former member of the group *Deep Purple.*

He has said he has seances to get closer to his god, and that while he performs he astro-projects out of his body to float around the concert hall (*Circus,* August 16, 1976, p. 30).

He records in a 17th-century castle supposedly haunted by a demon who is a servant of the 4,000-year-old Babylonian god, Baal (*Circus,* June 22, 1978, p. 15).

Ritchie said in a recent interview, "I am interested in odd things that happen, especially ghosts."

When asked if he liked to work in a ghostly atmosphere his reply was, "Yes, that's why I often take on castles when we rehearse and play. I don't like modern environment."

Later he went on to explain how he got involved in the occult.

"When we formed *Purple,* we had a bassist called Nic Simper. He used to do all these seances. I was totally opposed to all that, till I saw what was going on. I got intrigued with it all out of curiosity."

When asked what the ideal conditions were for holding a seance, he replied, "You can't be very tired. And you can't have weak personalities present: otherwise you'll get possession."

Later he explained, "A friend of mine, a guitarist, said, 'Ah I don't believe in all this rubbish. I'm not scared of you ghosts: I'm stronger than you are.' The next moment he was knocked out of his chair and was foaming at the mouth — he was unconscious. He had to go to a priest the next day and the priest said, 'Don't do that again: this is possession.

"You can go crazy if you're not careful," adds Blackmore. "A lot of people go too far too soon. . . ." (*Circus,* April 30, 1981, p. 45-46).

His occultic songs include "A Black Magician," "Stargazer" and "Tarot Woman" about the predictions of the occultic tarot cards. Ritchie Blackmore's music and message are certainly not that of a rainbow but rather a "Lake of Fire."

Chapter 15 — Part II

Behind the Faces

Blondie

Debbie Harry, former *Playboy* bunny and now the lead singer for *Blondie,* drifted into heroin addiction with her drummer boyfriend. When he died of an overdose, she went home to clean up her act (*US*, April 14, 1981, p. 71).

Debbie openly declares, "Rock and roll is all sex, 100 percent. Sometimes music can make you ————, which makes me ————. Most depends on the person. I don't know if people ———— ——— [masturbate] to my music. I hope so. I just dance around and shake . . . I wear tight clothes. I wear sexy clothes. I wear short skirts — try to look hot. If someone's undressing me with their eyes, that's not an offense to me. If someone's a pig, then that's horrible . . . but I don't think someone looking at me and envisioning me without my clothes is going to hurt me" (*Circus,* July 7, 1977, p. 40).

In a more recent interview she said, "I've always

thought that the main ingredients in rock are sex, really good stage shows, and really sassy music. Sex and sass; I really think that's where it's at" *(Hit Parader,* September 1979, p. 31).

She also has a live-in lover, Chris Stein, co-founder of the band *(US,* Par. 14, 1981, p. 70).

He adds in an interview, "Everybody takes it for granted, rock and roll is synonymous with sex" *(People,* May 21, 1979).

David Bowie

David Bowie was the first pop music star to openly proclaim his homosexuality.

He and his wife met while they were involved with the same man *(People,* August 18, 1975, p. 68).

Bowie has confessed to a deep involvement in drugs from heroin to cocaine.

He says, "Actually I was junked out of my mind most of the time. You can do good things with drugs but then comes the long decline" *(Rolling Stone,* January 12, 1978, p. 13).

He also stated "Rock and roll has always been the devil's music. It could well bring out a very evil feeling in the west" *(Rolling Stone,* February 12, 1976, p. 83).

He also bought a record player to play records backwards because he believes songs on his *Young Americans* album resemble Tibetan spiritualistic chants *(Hit Parader,* July 1975, p. 16).

His wife, Angela, was kicked out of a Connecticut college for being a lesbian (Bob Larson, *Rock).*

Eric Clapton

Eric has been given the title of the world's greatest living guitarist.

But he fell into a period of heroin addiction. He was

finally treated with acupuncture for his addiction.

Speaking of his drug experience, he said, "I had my first taste and thought, 'Oh, you know, one snort can't do me no harm!' But . . . dead wrong" (*Rolling Stone,* July 18, 1974, p. 54).

Captain and Tennille

Both share the same ideas and interests: ecology, vegetarian diets, a belief in reincarnation, karmic theory and your basic eternal bliss (*US,* September 16, 1980, p. 27).

Alice Cooper

Vincent Furnier, a Mormon preacher's son from Arizona, received his stage name while playing with a Ouija board. The board spelled out Alice Cooper and promised him world fame if he would change his name to the name of that 17th-century witch named Alice Cooper.

He later claimed to be the reincarnation of that 17th-century witch (*Circus,* December 19, 1978, p. 23).

He began his career coming on stage dressed as a transvestite in women's clothing. In his stage performances Alice smashes up life-like babies with blood capsules flying everywhere and at the end hangs himself on a gallows.

Alice has songs like "I Love the Dead," a song about necrophilia. Some of his other hits are "Cold Ethyl," "Welcome to My Nightmare," "Working Up a Sweat," and "Never Been Sold Before."

Other albums include *Billion Dollar Babies* and *Alice Cooper Goes to Hell.* All these hellish and sexual overtones that Alice uses don't make it very hard to believe that he is going to hell and leading many there along with him.

John Denver

The album *Rocky Mountain High* talks of a born-again experience by a man born in his 27th year.

In a *Newsweek* interview, Denver said, "As a self-appointed messiah, I view music as far more than just entertainment."

He said he sees it as a tool to promote the gospel of a new secular religion. The leaders of this religion claim to control the universe and "claim to be gods" (*Newsweek,* December 20, 1976).

In another song he says, "Apollo is the major deity of the sun, light, music and art" (*Symbols, Signs and Their Meanings,* A. Whittich, 1960, p. 190).

People Magazine interviewed Denver and revealed that he has tried Rolfing, Aikido, EST, Pyramid Power and other mystical religions, yet still feels fragmented (*People,* December 8, 1980, p. 65).

Doctor Hook

In 1972, perverted sex was put to a song by *Dr. Hook. Dr. Hook,* a seven-man hard rock band, had one song on the album called "Freakers Ball." It sings of a pervert convention. One part of the song says, "Come on babies, grease your lips, put on your hats and swing your hips. Don't forget to bring your whips (refers to sado-masochism), we're going to the freakers ball."

Verse two says you should bring your drugs, while verse three says what kind of people will be at the ball: "Fags" (homosexuals), "Dykes" (lesbians), "Leather freaks" (sadists, masochists) and "Junkies" (heroin addicts).

Doctor Hook in 1977 released an album entitled *Makin' Love and Music.* Songs included were, "Makin' Love and Music," "I Wanna Make the Woman Tremble," "Sexy

Energy," "Let the Loose End Drag," and "What a Way to Go."

One doesn't have to listen long to *Dr. Hook* to see their aim to destroy the morals of the youth today. Many who listen to them are sadly living out their perverted songs.

Eagles

The *Eagles* got their name from the major in the Indian Cosmos and many of their songs are nurtured by the drug peyote as well as being based on the teachings of Carlos Castenada, under whose occultic writings the band was formed *(Time,* August 15, 1975, p. 4).

Glen Fry of the *Eagles* said, "I am in the music business for sex and narcotics" *(People,* June 30, 1975, p. 30).

Ron Henley, 33, of the *Eagles,* was fined $2,500 and put on two years probation after pleading no contest to a charge of giving drugs to a 16-year-old girl found nude in his home last fall. He was sentenced in Santa Monica, California, on the misdemeanor charge of contributing to the delinquency of a minor *(Minneapolis Tribune,* February 26, 1981, p. 3a).

The *Eagles'* manager, Larry Salter, has admitted that members of the group had dealings with members of the satanic church, according to a Dallas evangelist who spoke with him *(Waco Tribune-Herald,* February 28, 1982).

Eagles' songs like "Take the Devil," "Journey of the Sorcerer," "Witchy Woman," "Good Day in Hell," "Hotel California" and "One of These Nights" (which lyrics say "You've got your demons, you've got your desires and I've got a few of my own") make very clear the occultic undercurrent that this group was based upon in its formation.

Earth, Wind and Fire

Maurice White, lead singer of the group, said, "The key to what's happening is, I think, recognizing self understanding — the powers that you have in yourself and allowing them to flow through you. Doing so you allow the magic to be viewed. I put that magic out and let people view it, dig, and not being afraid of allowing them to view it is the magic."

When asked if he thought he was in a previous incarnation he answered, "I don't know, I think it, my life, had something to do with what I'm doing now. Obviously it had something to do with the 900 years before Christ and the Egyptians and the Great Teachings and Africa and America. I think many times it's been in a teacher-type atmosphere" (*Circus,* January 19, 1978, p. 22).

When asked what kind of ritual they go through before going on stage, Maurice answered, "I hate to use the word 'ritual.' We do carry on before going on. We stand in a circle and hold hands and we basically kind of communicate to each other. We all say a prayer, each in our own way, and then we join the forces of harmony and go out and do what we do" (*Circus,* January 19, 1978, p. 23).

Maurice White is a practicing Buddhist (*Rolling Stone,* January 26, 1978, p. 14).

Their album *All n' All,* on the inside cover, shows different occultic beings on the same level as the cross of Christ.

The album *I Am* depicts a cross of Christ in the center with an embryo and an old man in the center with a temple to God in the foreground. Their song "Serpentine Fire" is based on the spinal life energy system found in Shah Kriza Yogi Meditation Cult.

Fleetwood Mac

Fleetwood Mac, had a hit-selling album *Rumours.* Their hit single on the album was a song "Rhiannon" who is a witch in Whales.

Stevie Nicks who sings the song also played the part of

"Rhiannon" in a movie (*Newsweek,* December 20, 1976).

Many times Stevie has been known to dedicate songs to "all the witches of the world."

Some of their music is published by the Welsh Witch Music.

Fleetwood Mac says they have received mail, baby announcements, from people who've named their daughters "Rhiannon" (*Circus,* April 14, 1977).

On the back of their album *Bare Trees* it says in the lower left-hand corner, "Special thanks to Mrs. Scarrot for her readings, recorded at her home in Hampshire."

"It's amazing cause sometimes when we're on stage," says Stevie, "I feel like somebody's just moving the pieces. Lindsey'll move back, I'll move forward. Christine will smile. Mick, then John, look over. I'm just going, 'God we don't have any control over this'; and that's magic.' "

That is the appeal of this band and that is what will make this band never be boring" (*Circus,* April 14, 1977, p. 41).

Stevie added in a later interview, "All these relationships between us are so close and they were so heavy, even in the beginning, that it's easy for me to think that we were together before in another life" (*Hit Parader,* April 1978, p. 4).

Rumours may be the hit album for *Fleetwood Mac,* but it is no rumor that this group is indulging in the occult; it is the bare facts.

Pink Floyd

This group's *Another Brick in the Wall, Part II,* soared right to the top of the charts.

Listen to some of the lyrics: "We don't need no education. We don't need no thought control. No dark sarcasm in the classroom. Teachers, leave the kids alone. Hey teachers, leave us kids alone."

Mind control? They have it over the minds of millions of young people as they encourage rebellion against authority in the school classrooms.

The Grateful Dead

The *Grateful Dead* evolved from a group known originally as the *Warlocks.*

Jerry Garcia, spokesman for the group, declared, "Acid rock is music you listen to when you are high on acid" (*Rolling Stone,* February 3, 1972, p. 30).

Robert Hunter, long time lyricist for the *Grateful Dead,* said in his ten commandments of rock and roll, "Destroy yourself physically and mentally and insist that all true brothers do likewise as an expression of unity" (*The Book of Rock Lists,* by Kevin Stein & Dave Marsh, p. 5).

The *Grateful Dead* were busted (arrested) for possession of narcotics (LSD and barbituates) in New Orleans, along with the celebrated LSD chemist Stanley Owsley, on January 31, 1970 (*The Book of Rock Lists,* p. 482).

Both Phil Leash, bassist for the *Grateful Dead,* and Jerry Garcia were busted at different times in 1973 for possession of drugs (*The Book of Rock Lists,* p. 482).

Ron (Pigpen) McKernan of the *Grateful Dead* died from accumulation of alcohol and drugs.

"Our lives are controlled by music," says Jerry Garcia (*People,* July 12, 1976, p. 50).

Phil Leash says about the group's lyrics, "A typical *Dead* lyric has just enough obscurity in it so that you're not really sure what it means" (*US,* August 5, 1980, p. 52-54).

A better name couldn't be given to this group to describe their music. I'm sure many will be grateful when their music is dead.

Top: The Iron Maiden's album *The Number of the Beast* is heavy into the black themes of the devil. *Bottom:* This album cover by the *Grateful Dead* speaks for itself.

Chapter 16 — Part 3

Behind the Faces

Hall N' Oates

Daryl Hall is a follower of Aleister Crowley and an admitted initiate of magic. He claims his song "Winged Bull" is dedicated to the ancient Celtic (witchcraft) religion *(Circus,* October 13, 1977, p. 28).

Daryl openly admits to being involved with witchcraft *(16 Magazine,* May 1981, p. 26).

Expressing his view on sex he said, "The idea of sex with a man doesn't turn me off. I had lots of strange experiences with older boys between when I was four and fourteen" *(Rolling Stone,* April 21, 1977, p. 15). *Hall 'N Oates* may seem very wholesome at first glance, but a further look into their lives shows them to be anything but wholesome.

Jimi Hendrix

Jimi Hendrix was born in 1942. He began playing the guitar at a young age. By the mid-sixties he had become a living legend.

When the *Monkeys* were at the peak of their career, Jimi toured with them as an opening act. Jimi would raise the guitar to his mouth and pluck the strings with his teeth. The performance climaxed at the end with Jimi setting the guitar on fire and beating it up against the amplifier.

Jimi was quoted as saying, "Rock is so much fun. That's what it's all about — filling up the chest cavities (smoking dope) and the empty kneecaps and elbows (shooting up)" (*The Book of Rock Lists,* Dave Marsh and Kevin Stein, p. 8).

Life Magazine quotes him as saying, "Atmospheres are going to come through music because music is a spiritual thing of its own. You can hypnotize people with music and when you get people at the weakest point you can preach into the subconscious what we want to say" (*Life,* October 3, 1969, p. 74).

He suffocated to death in 1970 afer an overdose of drugs.

Billy Joel

"I never do any drugs before a show. You can't do a two-and-a-half-hour show stoned," said Billy Joel. "Once I smoked pot before the show and when I walked on stage all I could say was 'What are you all doing here? Who am I? What is the meaning of life?' The guys in the band were going 'Oh boy!' Performing is like making love; you need to be at the height of your senses. One time I did some cocaine before a show. I ended up talking non-stop for a half hour. Finally my drummer came over and shut me up" (*Us,* June 24, 1980, p. 58).

Jimi Hendrix was a forerunner of the rock and roll mania that swept across America and around the world. He died of a drug overdose.

Jefferson Starship

Grace Slick of the group bore an illegitimate child and named it "god" with a small g. She said, "We've got to be humble about this" *(Newsweek,* February 8, 1971).

Grace, called by many the "Acid Queen of Rock and Roll," found motherhood slowed down her doping a bit. She said, "It's hard to keep an eye on the kid while you're hallucinating" *(People,* August 28, 1978, p. 72).

Guitarist Craig Chaquico said, "Rock concerts are the churches of today. Music puts them on a spiritual plane. All music is God" *(Bay Area Magazine,* February 1, 1977).

One song on the new *Jefferson Starship* album *Modern Times* is the song "Stairway to Cleveland." It has a chorus that says, "———— you, we do what we want."

Lead guitarist of the group, Paul Kanter, when asked how the group got their drugs, commented, "The group paid for it (the drugs). It was a business expense" *(Rolling Stone,* September 30, 1971, p. 30).

They had many drug-inspired songs like "White Rabbit" which was about heroin.

A warning to those interested in flying with *Jefferson Starship:* their flight pattern ends in death.

Jethro Tull

One of the Jethro Tull group members said, "If Jesus Christ came back today, he and I would get into our brown corduroys and go to the nearest jean store and overturn the racks of blue denim. Then we'd get crucified in the morning" *(Rolling Stone,* March 10, 1977, p. 13).

In the album *Aqualung* half of the songs about Jesus are filled with obscenities.

On the back of the album it says, "In the beginning man created God, and in the image of man created he him. And man gave unto him a multitude of names, that he

Top: **Grace Slick of *Jefferson Starship* is known as "the Acid Queen of Rock and Roll."** ***Bottom:*** **Unnatural sex is the theme of *REO Speedwagon's* album *Hi Infidelity.***

might be lord over all the earth when it was suited to man. And on the seventh millionth day man rested and did lean heavily on his God and said that it was good."

You can see that *Jethro Tull* has no respect for God and in many ways is anti-Christ; not in Christ's existence but his Lordship.

Elton John

Elton John, whose real name is Reg Dwight, has been hailed as an idol because of his musical genius.

Elton, at a glance, seems to be a soft-sounding rock star, but a second listen to his songs reveals his innermost thoughts.

His song "Bennie and the Jets" encourages teenage rebellion.

The song "Sweet Painted Lady" speaks of the virtues of prostitution. "All the Young Girls Love Alice" is a song about lesbians and his song "Bitch Is Back" is about sniffing glue.

Elton also admits he is both bisexual and suicidal, (*ROCK*, by Bob Larson, p. 132).

Bernie Taupin, former co-writer with Elton John, says Elton has a "home laden with trinkets and books relating to satanism and witchcraft" (*US*, July 22, 1980, p. 42).

Janis Joplin

Janis Joplin was born in Port Arthur, Texas. She, like Jimi Hendrix, died of a drug overdose at the peak of her career. Not only did they both die drug-related deaths, but both also died in 1970.

She declared her life goals in a *Time Magazine* interview: "I want to smoke dope, take dope, lick dope, anything I could get my hands on I wanted to do. All my life I just wanted to be a beatnik, meeting all the heavies, get stoned, get laid, have a good time'' *(Time,* August 9, 1969, p. 76).

About the music, Janis said, ''I couldn't believe it, all that rhythm and power. I got stoned just feeling it, like it was the best dope in the world. It was so sensual'' *(New York Times,* October 6, 1970).

Judas Priest

This English group's promotional material says that their new album *Sin After Sin* is selling sin or has sin for sale.

''*Judas Priest,* a new group from the industrial heartland of England is selling sin on their new album. Their new album is called *Sin After Sin,* but don't worry you will still be saved,'' the promotional piece says.

Of course the message of the album is that a person can live the way he wants to and still get by with it, still be saved.

KISS

Producer Bob Ezrin described *KISS* as ''symbols of unfettered evil and sensuality'' *(Rolling Stone,* March 25, 1976, p. 9).

KISS or ''Kids in Satan's Service'' *(American Photographer,* January 1980, p. 6) has been called by some rock magazines, ''Fire breathing demons from rock and roll hell.''

Peter Criss, while in *KISS,* said ''I find myself evil, I believe in the devil as much as God. You can use either one to get things done'' *(Rolling Stone,* April 7, 1977, p. 49).

Gene Simmons pointed out the values of *KISS* well when he said, ''The band is concerned with sex and little else'' *(Hard Rock,* June 1978, p. 62).

Chuck Pallard, a rock columnist, said, ''Just mention photography and he'll (Gene Simmons) drag out samples of

Top: **Janis Joplin, one of the hottest rock and roll stars ever, died of a drug overdose. A coroner's report said her body was eaten up with syphilis.** ***Bottom: KISS*** **(Kids in Service of Satan) is one of the most flagrantly vulgar groups around.**

his latest efforts, all of them terrific looking groupies who went all out for him while sharing his hotel suite" *(Hard Rock,* June 1978, p. 58; *People,* August 18, 1980).

Paul Stanley brags of what type of letters they have been getting, "Letters from 16-and 17-year-old girls with little Polaroid pictures of them naked. That's amazing! That's great! There's nothing like knowing you're helping the youth of America!"

Simmons relates in another interview, "I've always been interested in what human flesh tasted like and I've always wanted to be a cannibal. . . .

"If God is hot stuff then why is he afraid to have other gods before him? I've always wanted to be God" *(Circus,* September 13, 1976, p. 42).

Marvel Comics produced a special edition dedicated to *KISS.* Blood samples were taken from the group and smeared on the plates so they could literally say the comic was printed in the blood of the band *(ROCK,* by Bob Larson, p. 133).

Steve Gerber, *Marvel's* editor, aimed the magazine at eight- and nine-year-olds, stating that the decadence of *KISS* would enhance sales because the band appeals to "the base qualities of human nature."

Gerber went on, "At first their parents reaction will be total revulsion, then they'll shake their heads and go back to watching TV" *(Rocky Mountain News,* April 26, 1977).

On the album *Love Gun* one of the members of the group has his hand in a satanic salute. Their songs vary from the perverted "Sweet Pain" which is about sado-masochism, to "God of Thunder." This hellish song says "I gather darkness to please me and I command you to kneel before the god of thunder, the god of rock and roll."

Led Zeppelin

Led Zeppelin, called by many the most popular group in the world, has delved into the occult.

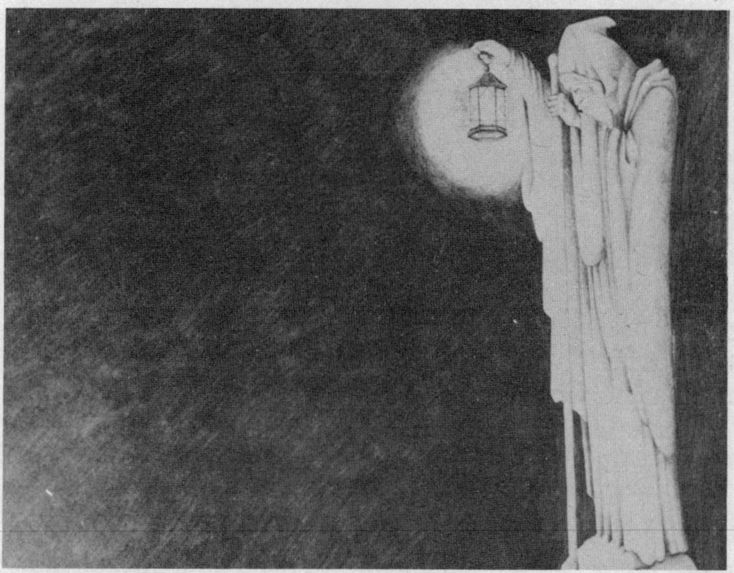

Top: Led Zeppelin's Stairway to Heaven **was one of the most popular albums of all time.** ***Bottom:*** **The inside cover of the album had this picture of "The Hermit," a tarot card symbol of the occult's wisdom and power.**

Robert Plant at one time confessed a fascination with the occult.

Jimmy Page, lead guitarist for the group, has been heavily involved in the occult as well as being a follower of black magician Aleister Crowley.

John "Bonzo" Bonham died after choaking on his own vomit in a drunken stupor.

Led Zeppelin has been a group that uses backward masking. For more information see the chapter titled "Stairway to Heaven?"

Meat Loaf

Jim Steinman, member of the group, says, "We've always been fascinated by the supernatural and always felt rock was the perfect idiom for it" (*Circus,* December 22, 1977, p. 12).

The lead singer of *Meat Loaf* adds, "When I go on stage, I get possessed" (*Time,* September 11, 1978).

Bette Midler

Since California state statutes were being changed at midnight to reduce the penalty for possession of small amounts of marijuana to a misdemeanor, Bette wanted to tape a joint to the bottom of every seat of the theatre where she was performing as a New Year's surprise.

Her staff had purportedly rolled 1,800 joints before word leaked out and the project was halted by the district attorney's office.

Still determined to give her audience something extra, at the stroke of midnight, goes the story, Bette dropped the top of her dress and manager Aaron Russo dropped the curtain (*Circus,* February 16, 1978, p. 42).

One of the performers in *Meat Loaf* says when he goes on stage he gets possessed.

Chapter 17 — Part IV

Behind the Faces

Iron Maiden

This group's latest album is titled *The Number of the Beast.* With songs like "Invaders" and "Children of the Damned" it makes one wonder as to what this band's appeal is.

"*Maiden* is far from a band of devil worshippers, although certain experiences they had while recording their latest album have taught them to respect the power of the occult" said one of the members of the group. "There were a lot of strange things going on while we were recording this record," he added. "In our new stage show, Eddie (the rotting corpse that serves as the band's mascot) comes on stage to do battle with the devil, and I can tell you that Eddie really kicks ———. It's *Maiden's* way of showing that rock and roll can overcome anything" *(Hit Parader,* Fall 1982, p. 27).

When asked if they were using the occult and horror as

a drawing card for the band, bassist Steve Harris replied, "I dunno about the occult because lemme make this clear . . . we're not 'into' the occult in the way that some other bands might be. I mean we don't go around casting spells or indulging in it" *(Creem,* September 1982, p. 61).

Barry McGuire

Barry McGuire was the prominent co-founder of the *Christie Minstrels.* While he was leading the *Minstrels* he recorded the group's first two-million seller entitled "Green, Green and Greenback Dollar."

Like so many others, he became disenchanted with the group and decided to try the rock music scene on his own.

One of his new songs — "Eve of Destruction" — was a forerunner of a great deal of protest music which has engulfed rock and roll.

The success of his new song catapulted him into a role of leadership within this country's counter culture.

Barry continued to gain national prominence as he played the lead male roll in the musical *Hair* which, of course, supposedly ushered in the dawn of a new age.

However, the real dawning of a new age took place in Barry's life when he met Jesus Christ and became a Christian.

After that encounter, his life-style and music changed as he lifted up the name of Jesus as Lord.

Jim Morrison

Jim Morrison of the *Doors* died at the age of 27.

Morrison said about his concerts, "I feel spiritual up there performing. Think of us as erotic politicians. I'm interested in anything about revolt, disorder, chaos, especially activity that has no meaning" *(Newsweek,* November 6,

1967, p. 101).

During his concert, according to charges filed by the State Attorney's office, "Morrison did lewdly and lasciviously expose his male genitals . . . and did unlawfully and publicly use and utter profane and indecent language" *(Newsweek,* April 7, 1969, p. 31).

Esquire Magazine had an interview with a young lady with whom Morrison had lived for some time. "He wanted dirty talk from me . . .," she said. "Sometimes . . . he would become violent, choking me and beating me. . . . Twice, I think, I was very close to getting killed" *(Esquire Magazine,* June 1972, p. 186).

Morrison's long-time girlfriend Pamela (who most people thought he had married by this time) lived upstairs from his former publicist Diane. One afternoon, Patricia, a house guest of Diane's, and one of Morrison's ex-girlfriends, confessed to Pamela that she had been pregnant with his child, but had an abortion.

At that moment Morrison came walking up the path and spied the two women in conversation. Pamela was terrified. That night Pamela waited for the axe to fall. Morrison refused to join her in bed, so she got drunk and went to sleep alone.

In the morning she "came downstairs and knocked on Diane's door. Diane came out of the bedroom, opened the door a crack and told Pamela 'I'm not going to deny that he's here.'

" 'I have only one thing to say to you and I'm gonna say it in front of all these people,' Pamela said. 'Jim, . . . you've ruined my Christmas. You spoil it for me every year. This is the fourth year you've done it.' "

Later Morrison put his arm around her and said, "It's all in the family" *(Hit Parader,* July 1982, p. 261).

Nazareth

Nazareth released two albums — *Hair of the Dog* and *Expect No Mercy* — and both album covers featured demon manifestations. Some observers believe that the artist who painted the pictures for the cover of the album must have been well acquainted with the occult.

This is another example of how rock and roll groups are heavy into the occult, black magic, witchcraft and even Satan worship.

However, many teenagers aren't mature enough to make the connection and thus open their minds to spiritual pollution.

Ted Nuggent

In an interview with Scott Cohen in *Circus Magazine* Ted Nuggent said, ". . . killed a raccoon, scraped it off the pavement, brought it home with me, skinned it, boiled it and ate it." *Circus Magazine* reported that 12 people died in a riot after a performance in South Carolina *(Circus,* May 13, 1976, p. 29).

Ted Nuggent's performances are more than an act. His perverted songs come from a perverted life-style.

Ozzy Osbourne

As *Black Sabbath's* frontman until 1979, Osbourne was one of the first rock singers to link an image of satanic power with the gut-wrenching kick of the music he performs *(Circus,* July 31, 1982, p. 35).

Since being on his own he has released two albums. One *The Blizzard of Ozz* and his latest *Diary of a Mad Man.*

On one of his albums he has a song titled "Mr. Crowley" referring to Aleister Crowley, the late satanist who

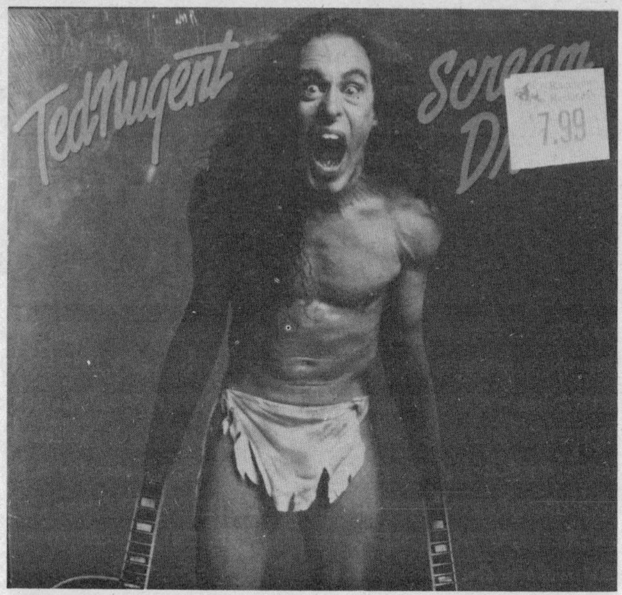

Top: **Ted Nuggent has been called "The Madman of Detroit."** ***Bottom: Uriah Heap's*** **album** ***Abominog*** **has demonic overtones.**

reportedly had human sacrifices in his home.

Osbourne claims he was compelled to see the movie "The Exorcist" 26 times (*Circus,* February 1976).

Osbourne was quoted as saying, "I don't know if I'm a medium for some outside force or not. Frankly, whatever it is I hope it's not what I think it is, Satan" (*Hit Parader,* February 1978, p. 24).

Osbourne also said in a recent interview, "No matter what you do, you've got to admit that there are certain minority groups in America that always want to screw things up for other people — always want to stop people from enjoying themselves. And the thing is they can't because rock and roll is a religion in itself. What's wrong with it?" (*The Times-Picayune,* August 6, 1982).

Osbourne received precautionary treatment for rabies after biting off the head of a bat at a recent concert (*Waco Tribune-Herald,* January 28, 1982).

He was committed to a London sanitarium for, according to his exasperated manager, "taking all his clothes off in a record company board meeting . . . (*Hit Parader,* April 1982, p. 26).

The Police

The Police is the new hit sensation from England. With their newly proclaimed "sex symbol" bassist Sting, they have become one of the many uprising new groups from overseas.

Sting said in a recent interview, "We'll probably get into drugs and Eastern mysticism to get our songs. In fact some of us already are" (*Creem,* July/August 1982, p. 32).

They already have one song which refers to the Eastern religion Zen.

My caution about this group is simple and practical: watch out for *The Police.*

Prince

This group's *Dirty Mind* album cover portrays the hero dressed in a trench coat and black bikini staring somberly into the camera.

Interwoven through two of the major tunes "Party-Up" and "Uptown" are such themes as bisexuality and incest, according to *Rolling Stone Magazine,* February 19, 1981.

The language in the *Prince* songs is so vulgar it should have a warning label on the cover — and it does! The warning simply admits that the song "Uptown" is perverted.

One *Prince* member said, "When I brought it (Uptown) to the record company it shocked a lot of people, but they didn't ask me to go back and change anything and I'm really grateful."

Queen

The name comes from a slang word meaning homosexual.

Freddie Mercury, the lead singer of the group, is the one featured. During a concert Mercury is in full make-up from finger nail polish to mascara strips down from his skin-tight pants to his tight hot pants. It's not hard to see the group's bisexual appeal. Mercury once said, "We want to shock and be outrageous" (*Circus,* April 1974, p. 41).

Their album *Jazz* was promoted by *Queen* sponsorship of a nude bicycle race in which 55 people entered.

Drummer Roger Taylor calls the group's latest album *Hot Space* "intelligently dirty."

Lead singer and friend of tightsmakers, Freddie Mercury, helped formulate the nude body design for the single sleeve of "Body Language" which has already been censored by certain retailers. "Body Language" is stripped down to the gears, its lyrics direct enough to steam your windows *(Hit Parader,* October 1982, pp. 60-61). Freddie confesses, "I think I may go mad in several years time" *(Circus,* March 1977, p. 42). *Queen's* song "We Are the Champions" has been widely interpreted as the anthem of the Gay Liberation.

Patty Smith

Patty says one of her goals is to write rock and roll pornography.

Lesbianism is one of the themes in her music.

Some of her lyrics goes like this: "Oh, she looks so fine. I've got this crazy feeling I'm gonna make her mine." This is clearly and simply one girl singing about another girl.

According to *Circus Magazine,* February 10, 1976, Patty introduces her song "Redondo Beach" as "A new song about a beach where women love women."

Her songs are also laced with such themes as lust, death, dreams and demons.

Her album *Horses* has a poem which says, "Jesus died for somebody's sins but not mine. My sins are my own, they belong to me."

REO Speedwagon

This group came to world acclaim when the album *Hi-Infidelity* (which means to be sexually unfaithful to your spouse) sold some six million copies.

The album cover shows a woman who appears to be a prostitute. But this is not an unfamiliar theme to Kevin Cronin who claims, "The main reason I got into rock and roll was to meet girls."

Such ladies have been a source both of song ideas and of trouble with his wife — the kind of cheating and making up that inspired "Keep on Loving You."

"I like living on the edge," he adds (*Circus,* August 31, 1982, p. 32).

"We started out playing bars, then we got too big for playing bars so we moved on to playing high schools, then we got too big for high schools, so we went on to colleges, et cetera . . . until now where we're getting too big to play stadiums.

"And by now," Kevin Cronin laughed, adding the punch line, "we have a cult of three million people following us. . . . We were held back by things we couldn't control, like producers."

Rolling Stones

Mick Jagger of the *Rolling Stones* says "All dancing is a replacement for sex" (*G.Q. Scene,* Spring 1967, p. 72). "He says that his first sexual experience was a homosexual and confesses a desire for his own daughter to have sex at an early age" (*People,* October 3, 1977, p. 108).

Richard Oldham, their manager, declared, "Rock music is sex and you have to hit them (teenagers) in the face with it" (*Time,* April 28, 1967, p. 72).

Oldham admits the *Stones* were all heavily into drugs. (Brian Jones of the *Stones* drowned in his swimming pool as a direct result of an overdose). Oldham says that at the well-publicized drug bust, the *Stones* were just coming down from a 12-hour acid trip (*Rolling Stone,* August 19, 1972, p. 30). He adds, "There are black magicians who think we are acting as unknown agents of Lucifer, and others who think we are Lucifer," (*Rolling Stone,* August 19, 1971).

Even *Newsweek Magazine* called Mick Jagger "The Lucifer of rock, the unholy roller," and spoke of his demonic power to affect people (January 4, 1971, p. 44).

Speaking of his performances, Jagger says, "You can feel the adrenalin going through your body . . ." (*News-*

week, January 4, 1971, p. 47).

Another time he described his performances by admitting, "I entice my audience. What I do is very much the same as a girl's striptease dance" (*G.Q. Scene,* Spring, 1967, p. 72).

Keith Richards once observed that the *Stones'* songs came spontaneously, like inspiration at a seance. He explains that the tunes arrive "en masse" as if the *Stones* as songwriters are only a willing and open medium (*Rolling Stone,* May 5, 1977, p. 55).

Anita Pallenberg, Keith Richards' live-in girlfriend, was involved in the occult and even cast a spell that brought death to a young man. Kenneth Anger was her teacher in the occult. Anger is a disciple of Aleister Crowley. Anger's life work was the film, "Lucifer's Rising."

Hired to play the part of Lucifer in the movie was Bobby Beausoleil, a guitarist for the California rock band *Love.'* Mysteriously after many months of filming, Bobby went beserke and carried out a singularly beastial murder which ended with his writing on a wall with his victim's blood (*Up and Down with the Rolling Stones,* by Tony Sanchez, pp. 45-47).

"Goats Head Soup" was partially recorded at a Haitian voodoo ritual. The goat head is a universal symbol for satanism.

The Stones' album title *Get Yer Ya-Yas Out* is based on a phrase which recurs frequently in African voodoo.

The song "Black N' Blue" was advertised in California on a huge billboard with a young lady tied down being beaten by her lovers.

In the song "Dancin' with Mr. D," Mr. D is the devil. The song "Sympathy for the Devil" is an unofficial national anthem for all satanic churches in America.

All of the *Stones* are heavily involved in drugs. Bianca Jagger, Mick's ex-wife, recently told *Parade Magazine* that she'd still be married to ol' rubber lips if he hadn't had so many affairs. "Mick was desolate when it came to women," she said (*Creem,* September 1982, p. 13).

The Who

The Who is a revolutionary group that, since its beginning in the 60's, have become a legend.

Pete Townsend is known best for beating his guitar on the ground and against the amplifier until it is destroyed.

Townsend is a follower of the Eastern Mystic Meher Baba. He says, "Rama Krishna, Buddha, Zarathustra, Jesus and Meher Baba are all divine figures on earth. They all said basically the same thing; yet we still trundle on" (*"The Who" in Their Own Words,* compiled by Steve Clarke).

Townsend has written songs on their albums dedicated to Meher Baba. All members of the group have been involved in drugs.

Keith Moon, drummer of the group, died of drug-related circumstances.

Pete Townsend was quoted as saying, "Pop (or rock) has become solemn, irrelevant, and boring. What it needs now is more noise, more size, more sex, more violence, more gimmickery, more vulgarity. Above all, it desperately needs a new messiah who will take things right back to the glamour, power and insanity of the Elvis Presley age" (*Book of Rock Lists,* by Dave Marsh and Kevin Stein, p. 6).

Recently 85,000 young fans packed the Los Angeles Coliseum to watch *The Who* perform.

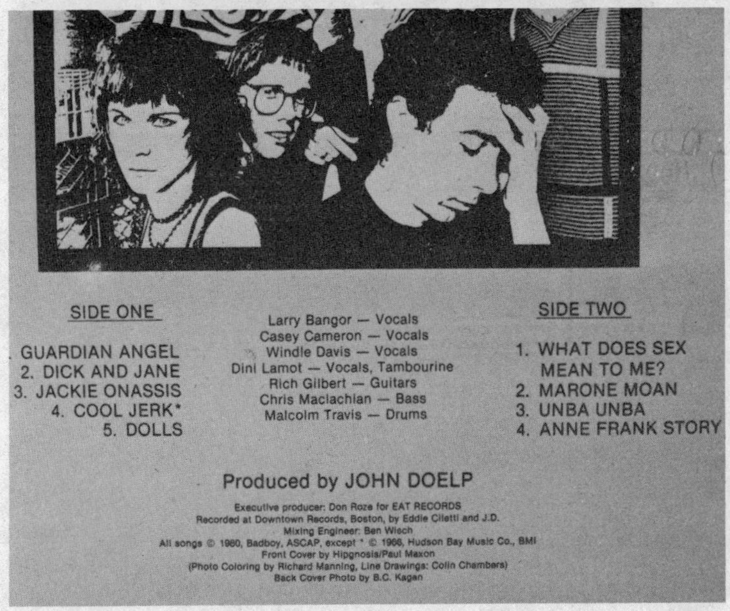

Here is both the front and back covers of *Human Sexual Response* which even attempts to exploit little children.

Dr. John is a licensed witch.

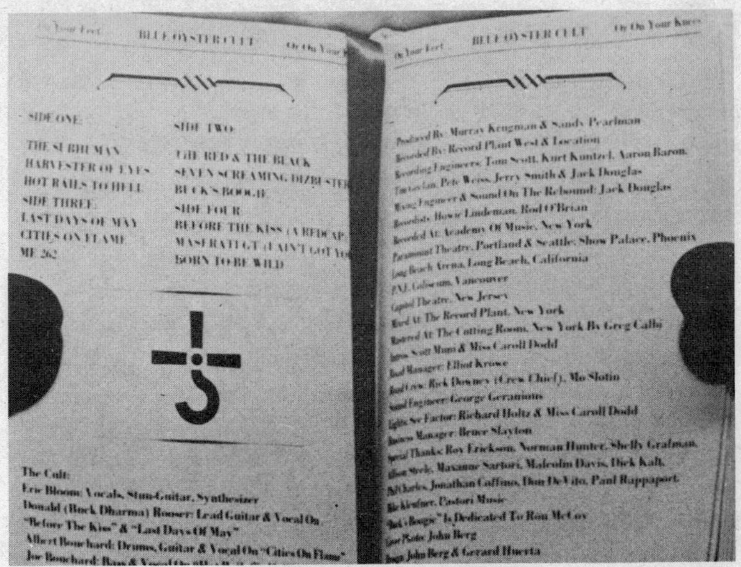

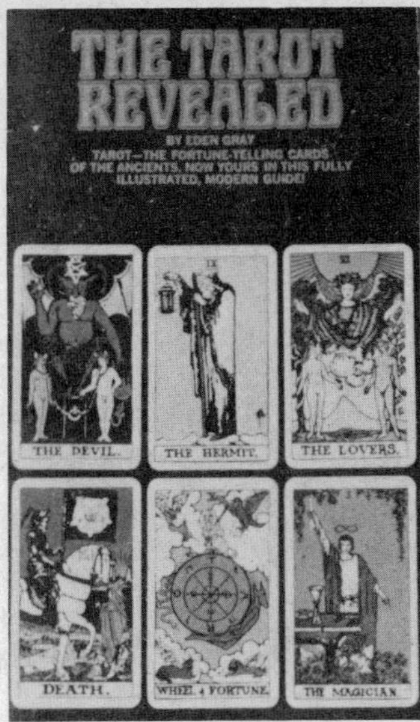

Top: **This is the back of the album cover by the *Blue Oyster Cult.* Notice the Antichrist symbol — the cross with the question mark. It asks: What really happened at the cross? *Bottom:* This book *The Tarot Revealed* is a handbook on the occult.**

Thousands of teenagers — like the ones above — have become so disenchanted and disgusted with rock and roll music that they have conducted hundreds of album-burnings all across America. They openly break all ties with rock music and its strong emphasis on unnatural sex, drugs, and the occult.

Chapter 18

My Song

I can never really remember not being around music.

My sisters sang and so did my brother. My sisters were even going to record an album at one time, but my dad thought it would lead to their dropping out of school so he didn't let them. They dropped out anyway!

As far back as I can remember they were listening to Frankie Valle, Neil Sadaka and others playing similar music.

I was always more influenced by my brother who was listening to the *Beatles, Poco, Jefferson Starship* and the *Rolling Stones.* He once spent the night outside a concert hall just go get tickets to a *Rolling Stones* concert.

The crowd that I ran with was just beginning to get into people like Janis Joplin, *Black Sabbath, The Guess Who, Led Zeppelin* and, my favorite, Jimi Hendrix. Although I never saw him in concert I treasured every picture, poster or album that I had of him.

I believe we could have titled it the "Age of Black

Lights." Because of the fluorescent lighting fad we bought black light T-shirts, black light posters, black light pants, black light shoes . . . you name it and we either had it or could get it!

Psychedelics were in and words like "far out, heavy, solid, and wow" were in their prime. It seemed the whole world was taking acid, snorting THC, and dropping mescalin.

All the one-time flower children were so stoned that all they could see was flowers. There were peace signs on everything — clothes, street signs, cars, trees, sides of stores, everywhere! I was 14 years old in the midst of it all.

At home everybody was playing their role. Nobody was on drugs. Everybody was happy and we were all fit to be the next guests on the Ozzie and Harriet show!

But the youth of America were in the prime of their rebellion.

With rock and roll in my ears, and drugs in my mind, I was trying to understand my role in this messed-up world.

My family, like many others, had been through a divorce. The only place I really felt comfortable was out on the streets. I was living with my dad and stepmother who was a "backslidden Pentecostal woman preacher." My friends and I were into the street gangs and we thought stealing and violence was where it was at.

As if all this wasn't bad enough, they had just started integration in the schools. Because our school was 90-percent Mexican a lot of integration was to come its way.

By the time it was all over we ended up with a school that was 60 percent Mexican, 39 percent black and one percent white! Our school already had problems with drugs, sex and violence. All integration did for our school was put the match to the fuse of a bomb that was already there.

We began to have race riots. All the blacks were running around saying, "We's want black power." The Mexicans were running around saying, "Hey dude, we want

Chicano power." The whites were just running around saying, "We want OUT!"

The principal had been beaten up three times that year. Many teachers feared the students and knew that they couldn't control them.

It was at this time that a man drove by the school with the desire to reach out to the school. It was as if God spoke to him and said, "I've given it to you. Go and tell the principal." So he pulled over and went in and told the principal what had happened and that he wanted to preach to the students.

"What can you do for our school? Teachers are afraid to even stay in the classrooms! What can you possibly do? Anyway it's against the law to preach in schools," the principal said.

But the thing was that this man knew what Jesus could do for the school and he was able to convince the hopeless principal to allow him an hour's time during the student assembly.

As a result of this man's arrival at our school of 2,500 students, within a week's time over 1,000 of the students gave their lives to Christ.

Our school turned into a revival center! Instead of carrying knives and chains, they began to carry Bibles! You could see T-shirts throughout the classrooms that read "Read your Bible. It will scare the hell out of you!"

Needless to say I was one of the 1,000 who gave their lives to Christ. I left drugs, gangs, sex and rock and roll behind me.

But in the midst of all this I had no idea of the great adventure that God had in store for me! When I went home and told my father and stepmother what had happened to me, they were shocked. The Mormonism, which was the prevailing religion in our home at the time, conflicted with my Christianity.

Through a series of run-ins with my parents I was forced to move out of the house. The only one I had to turn to was my real mom. I then called her up and told her my story. She said I could come live with her and I left with the address she had given. What a shock to find her residence with a big sign reading "The Parres Lounge!" Little did I know that would be my home for the next three years!

I had to serve beer while living there. Even though it looked like a bad situation, God really used it for good because that's where I began to preach. I was able to share Christ with many drunks, drug addicts and prostitutes.

The amazing part is that God kept me straight every day that I lived there. Never did I drink or get involved with my past life.

The Bible says, "As many as received him (Jesus), to them he gave the power to become the sons of God."

Today, if you don't know Christ as your Lord, the Supreme ruler of your life, you can! You're lost without him! You might say "Well I don't know if I'm lost or not."

A friend of mine and I were walking through a carnival and he said, "Let's go and get lost in a mirror house."

I said, "You know being lost and being in a mirror house have a lot in common. Because when you're lost all you can see is yourself."

Let me share with you four things you must know about your life today:

1. Do you know what you must do to be a candidate for hell? Nothing! No response to the call of Christ on your life IS a response, you reject him.

2. You might say, "Well I'm a good person." This may be true; but Jesus never came to make bad men good. He came to make dead men live. If you have never totally committed your life to Christ then you are dead spiritually.

3. "Well I've got God in my plans." Yes, you may. But do you have the plan of God? Remember, he's God, not you. If you are still seeking your own happiness with your plan, then you are the god of your life.

4. "Well I love God and believe in Jesus and will commit my life to him someday, but not now." You cannot commit your life to Christ whenever you like. The Bible says, "No man can come unto God unless the Spirit draws him." If God's Spirit is dealing with you, the time is now. The Bible also says, "Today is the day of Salvation." DON'T WAIT!

"How do I receive Christ?"

1. Admit that you are a sinner and that you have been ruling your own life; that you've stolen it from its rightful owner . . . its Creator (Romans 3:23).
2. Ask God to forgive your sin and selfish way of living. This is called repentance which means to receive a change of heart. Instead of living selfishly for yourself you will begin to live for God and others, which will produce genuine happiness in your life.
3. Realize that the only way to God is through his Son Jesus Christ the Lord. Ask him to come into your life like you would ask anyone into your home (read John chapter 3).

CAUTION: Remember with Jesus it's all of your life or nothing!

MURDERED HEIRESS . . . LIVING WITNESS, by Dr. Petti Wagner, $5.95.

This is the book of the year about Dr. Petti Wagner — heiress to a large fortune — who was kidnapped and murdered for her wealth, yet through a miracle of God lives today.

Dr. Wagner did indeed endure a horrible death experience, but through God's mercy, she had her life given back to her to serve Jesus and help suffering humanity.

Some of the events recorded in the book are terrifying. But the purpose is not to detail a violent murder conspiracy but to magnify the glorious intervention of God.

THE HIDDEN DANGERS OF THE RAINBOW: The New Age Movement and Our Coming Age of Barbarism, by Constance Cumbey, $5.95.

A national best-seller, this book exposes the New Age Movement which is made up of tens of thousands of organizations throughout the world. The movement's goal is to set up a one-world order under the leadership of a false christ.

Mrs. Cumbey is a trial lawyer from Detroit, Michigan, and has spent years exposing the New Age Movement and the false christ.

Feel Better and Live Longer Through **THE DIVINE CONNECTION,** by Dr. Donald Whitaker.

This is a Christian's guide to life extension. Dr. Whitaker of Longview, Texas, says you really can feel better and live longer by following Biblical principles set forth in the word of God.

THE DIVINE CONNECTION shows you how to experience divine health, a happier life, relief from stress, a better appearance, a healthier outlook, a zest for living and a sound emotional life. And much, much more.

THE AGONY OF DECEPTION, by Ron Rigsbee with Dorothy Bakker, $6.95.

Ron Rigsbee was a man who through surgery became a woman and now through the grace of God is a man again. This book — written very tastefully — is the story of God's wondrous grace and His miraculous deliverance of a disoriented young man. It offers hope for millions of others trapped in the agony of deception.

THE DAY THEY PADLOCKED THE CHURCH, by E. Edward Rowe, $3.50.

The warm yet heartbreaking story of Pastor Everett Sileven, a Nebraska Baptist pastor, who was jailed and his church padlocked because he refused to bow to Caesar. It is also the story of 1,000 Christians who stood with Pastor Sileven in defying Nebraska tyranny in America's crisis of freedom.

BACKWARD MASKING UNMASKED/Backward Satanic Messages of Rock and Roll Exposed, by Jacob Aranza, $4.95.

Are rock and roll stars using the technique of backward masking to implant their own religious and moral values into the minds of young people? Are these messages satanic, drug-related and filled with sexual immorality? Jacob Aranza answers these and other questions.

SCOPES II/THE GREAT DEBATE, by Louisiana State Senator Bill Keith, 193 pages, $4.95.

Senator Keith's book strikes a mortal blow at evolution, which is the cornerstone of the religion of secular humanism. He explains what parents and others can do to assure that creation science receives equal time in the school classrooms, where Christian children's faith is being destroyed.

WHY J.R.? A Psychiatrist Discusses the Villain of Dallas, by Dr. Lew Ryder, 152 pages, $4.95.

An eminent psychiatrist explains how the anti-Christian religion of secular humanism has taken over television programming and what Christians can do to fight back.

NEED A MIRACLE? by Harald Bredesen, 159 pages, $4.95.

This book shows how to draw upon the greatest power in the universe to cope with "unsolvable" problems; "incurable" illnesses; enslaving habits; and day-to-day money shortages.

YES, LORD! by Harald Bredesen, 198 pages, $4.95.

This is a wonderful story of God's power and grace. Pat Boone said: "Knowing Harald Bredesen is a little like knowing Elijah. Miracles follow him wherever he goes."